CliffsNotes™

A Farewell to Arms

By Adam Sexton, M.F.A.

IN THIS BOOK

- Learn about the Life and Background of the Author
- Preview an Introduction to the Novel
- Study a graphical Character Map
- Explore themes and literary devices in the Critical Commentaries
- Examine in-depth Character Analyses
- Enhance your understanding of the work with Critical Essays
- Reinforce what you learn with CliffsNotes Review
- Find additional information to further your study in CliffsNotes Resource Center and online at www.cliffsnotes.com

D0062264

Wiley Publishing, Inc.

About the Author
Adam Sexton is a teacher and freelance writer. He received a B.A. in English from the University of Pennsylvania and an M.F.A. in Writing from Columbia University. He lives in Brooklyn, New York.

Publisher's Acknowledgments
Editorial
Project Editor: Tracy Barr
Acquisitions Editor: Greg Tubach
Glossary Editors: The editors and staff at Webster's New World™ Dictionaries
Editorial Administrator: Michelle Hacker
Production
Indexer: York Production Services, Inc.
Proofreader: York Production Services, Inc.
Wiley Publishing, Inc., Indianapolis Composition Services

CliffsNotes™ *A Farewell to Arms*

Published by:
Wiley Publishing, Inc.
909 Third Avenue
New York, NY 10022
www.wiley.com

Copyright © 2001 Wiley Publishing, Inc., New York, New York

Library of Congress Control Number: 00-107678

ISBN: 0-7645-8659-9

Printed in the United States of America

10 9 8 7 6 5 4

1O/TQ/QX/QS/IN

Published by Wiley Publishing, Inc., New York, NY
Published simultaneously in Canada

Table of Contents

How to Use This Book

CliffsNotes *A Farewell to Arms* supplements the original work, giving you background information about the author, an introduction to the novel, a graphical character map, critical commentaries, expanded glossaries, and a comprehensive index. CliffsNotes Review tests your comprehension of the original text and reinforces learning with questions and answers, practice projects, and more. For further information on Ernest Hemingway and *A Farewell to Arms*, check out the CliffsNotes Resource Center.

CliffsNotes provides the following icons to highlight essential elements of particular interest:

Reveals the underlying themes in the work.

Helps you to more easily relate to or discover the depth of a character.

Uncovers elements such as setting, atmosphere, mystery, passion, violence, irony, symbolism, tragedy, foreshadowing, and satire.

Enables you to appreciate the nuances of words and phrases.

Don't Miss Our Web Site

Discover classic literature as well as modern-day treasures by visiting the CliffsNotes Web site at www.cliffsnotes.com. You can obtain a quick download of a Cliffs-Notes title, purchase a title in print form, browse our catalog, or view online samples.

You'll also find interactive tools that are fun and informative, links to interesting Web sites, tips, articles, and additional resources to help you, not only for literature, but for test prep, finance, careers, computers, and the Internet too. See you at www.cliffsnotes.com!

LIFE AND BACKGROUND OF THE AUTHOR

Formative Years

Ernest Hemingway was born on July 21, 1899, in Oak Park, Illinois, a prosperous suburb of Chicago that was also home to the American architect Frank Lloyd Wright. His father, Clarence E. Hemingway, was a doctor; his mother, who was very religious, had given up a promising career as a singer in order to rear six children, of whom Ernest was the third and the oldest boy.

Hemingway attended public school in Oak Park, and the family vacationed in the north woods of Michigan, where Clarence taught Ernest hunting and fishing and a general love of the outdoor life. Later Hemingway would portray Oak Park's bourgeois values in an unflattering light in stories like "Soldier's Home," and his parents' marriage was the subject of the bitterly resentful tale "The Doctor and the Doctor's Wife." On the other hand, Hemingway wrote with nothing short of adoration about life "Up in Michigan," in the story of that name and many others featuring his fictional alter ego Nick Adams. Clarence Hemingway would commit suicide in 1928.

Upon graduation from high school, Hemingway left Oak Park for a stint as a reporter at the highly respected daily newspaper the *Kansas City Star*. Shortly afterward, he enlisted in a Red Cross ambulance corps stationed on the Austrian front in Italy during the last year of the First World War. Hemingway was wounded almost immediately (he was delivering cigarettes and chocolate to Italian soldiers beyond the front lines) and sent to an American hospital in Milan, where he fell in love with an American nurse named Agnes von Kurowsky; these events would inspire *A Farewell to Arms*. After the war, Hemingway returned to the States in hopes of beginning a career of one kind or another that would support him and Agnes, whom he planned to marry. That plan was shattered when she wrote from Europe to say that she'd fallen in love with another man.

Instead, Hemingway married Hadley Richardson in 1921; shortly thereafter, the couple moved to Paris, where the first of the writer's three sons was born. All the while, Hemingway was reading as much as he could, writing stories and poems, and trying to find his voice as a writer—a process that suffered a devastating setback when a suitcase containing all the copies of all the stories he had written to date (four years' work) was stolen from Hadley on a train to Switzerland.

Education

Hemingway's formal education did not extend beyond high school in Oak Park, where he edited the school paper. His training as a writer continued, however, during his time as a reporter in Kansas City and as a foreign correspondent for the *Toronto Star*. He covered the Greek-Turkish War of 1920, and the experience would inspire some of the most striking and effective of the inter-chapter vignettes in Hemingway's groundbreaking debut story collection, *In Our Time*.

Even more influential, perhaps, were the writers Hemingway met while living in Paris during the 1920s: the Irishman James Joyce and the American expatriates Ezra Pound, F. Scott Fitzgerald, and especially Gertrude Stein. Hemingway liked to claim that he learned about writing from the post-Impressionist paintings of Cezanne—an intriguing notion, though he never made it clear exactly what Cezanne taught him.

Any discussion of Hemingway's education would be incomplete without a mention of the attention and energy he devoted to the subject matter of his books. Just as he learned to write from the most talented contemporary practitioners of the craft, he apprenticed himself to acknowledged experts in warfare and the "blood sports" with which his work is so often concerned. He learned about military tactics from career soldiers met in World War I, bullfighting from Spanish matadors, big-game hunting from a British guide in East Africa, and deep-sea fishing from a native of the Bahamas. Hemingway loved mastering the abstruse terminology and complex procedures of each of these activities. As any reader of his work knows, he also was fascinated by food and drink; the pages of Hemingway's fiction and nonfiction are filled to overflowing with references to foreign dishes and obscure wines and liqueurs. Finally, he was a quick study at languages and was relatively fluent in quite a few.

Literary Writing

Hemingway's first book published in the United States, *In Our Time* (1925), was a collection of stories (like "Indian Camp" and "Big Two-Hearted River") linked by the character of Nick Adams, who appears in many of them; by the short vignettes between the stories that tell a story of their own; by the theme of behavior in the face of life-threatening violence; and by the now-famous Hemingway style. The book was acclaimed upon its publication, and it remains a classic.

The Torrents of Spring, a novella that attempts in a rather belabored fashion to satirize the work of the American writer Sherwood Anderson, followed in 1926, as did Hemingway's *The Sun Also Rises*, a novel about expatriate life in Paris and Spain after World War I. In both subject and style, the latter book is a genuinely radical work of Modern art. (The specifics of its central conflict are never explicitly stated, for instance.) *The Sun Also Rises* is probably the most-admired of all the writer's books. *Men Without Women* (1927) comprises stories of boxers and bullfighters, including "The Undefeated," "The Killers," and "Fifty Grand." *Men Without Women* also contains "Hills Like White Elephants," a story told almost entirely in dialogue.

Published in 1929, *A Farewell to Arms* toned down Hemingway's revolutionary style to yield a more conventional—and a more moving—book than the writer had produced up to that time. The result was the novel's widespread popular success as well as worldwide fame for the author himself. The story collection *Winner Take Nothing* followed in 1933. Less consistently satisfying than the two collections that preceded it, *Winner Take Nothing* nevertheless contained more formal experimentation, like the verbatim foreign dialogue in "Wine of Wyoming."

At this point in his career, Hemingway seems to have become distracted by his own celebrity. Eight years would pass between *A Farewell to Arms* and the writer's next novel, the slight and poorly received *To Have and Have Not* (1937)—which is really a collection of linked short stories that share a setting (Cuba and Key West) rather than a true novel. In the interim, Hemingway wrote two books of nonfiction: a loose, baggy treatise on bullfighting called *Death in the Afternoon* (1932) and *The Green Hills of Africa* (1935), which was about big-game hunting. All the while, the Hemingway legend was growing, thanks in no small part to the author's own embellishments (and sometimes out-and-out lies) about his past.

Finally, in 1940, *For Whom the Bell Tolls* appeared. The book is a big novel about the Spanish Civil War, which Hemingway had covered as a correspondent and documentary filmmaker. Critics accused it, and him, of self-parody—and indeed, the novel's style is often unbearably mannered. Still, the best-selling *For Whom the Bell Tolls* stands among the early stories and his first two novels as Hemingway's main storytelling achievements.

During the Second World War, Hemingway occupied himself by reporting from Europe. In 1950, he published another book, the critically lambasted *Across the River and Into the Trees*. He recovered somewhat with *The Old Man and the Sea* (1952), a novella about a Cuban fisherman's struggle with a great marlin, which might be Hemingway's answer to *Moby-Dick*. His most popular work, *The Old Man and the Sea* was the last Ernest Hemingway book to be published before the author's suicide in Ketchum, Idaho, on July 2, 1961. *A Moveable Feast*, his charming memoir of the years spent with other expatriates in Paris during the 1920s, appeared three years later.

Hemingway's fame, and the public's desire for more of his work, continues to be so formidable that his executors have brought out a number of books since his death that the writer himself had not considered fit for publication. *Islands in the Stream* (1970) reprises *To Have and Have Not*'s Caribbean setting. *The Garden of Eden* (1986), about a *menage a trois*, dramatizes the author's fascination with androgyny hinted at in *The Sun Also Rises* and near the end of *A Farewell to Arms*, as well as in stories like "The Sea Change." *The Complete Short Stories: The Finca Vigia Edition* (1987) contains some of the author's unpublished short fiction. And 1999's *True at First Light* either reports on or imagines an affair between a Hemingway-like hero and an African girl.

Honors and Awards

The most influential American writer of the twentieth century, Ernest Hemingway was rewarded throughout his life for his achievements. Upon the appearance of his first published stories, he received the kudos of his literary peers, giants like James Joyce and Ezra Pound. With the publication of *A Farewell to Arms*, he achieved bestsellerdom. By the time *For Whom the Bell Tolls* appeared, "Papa" Hemingway was recognized worldwide by millions who had never read a word of his prose; he had achieved a degree of celebrity that had never been approached by a literary writer and has not been matched since.

Near the end of his life, the adulation was made explicit, as *The Old Man and the Sea* was awarded the Pulitzer Prize in 1953. The following year, Hemingway won the Nobel Prize for Literature "for his powerful, style-forming mastery of the art of narration." Though his popularity has diminished somewhat in the past quarter-century due to charges of sexism and brutality in his life and work, Ernest Hemingway's influence lives on. Whether consciously or not, any writing teacher who advises students to "show, don't tell" is paying Hemingway tribute.

INTRODUCTION TO THE NOVEL

Introduction

A Farewell to Arms is not a complicated book. Rather, it is a simple story well told, the plot of which could be summarized as follows: boy meets girl, boy gets girl, boy loses girl. Ernest Hemingway conveyed this story chronologically, in a strictly linear fashion, with no flashback scenes whatsoever. In fact, the novel contains very little exposition at all. We never learn exactly where its narrator and protagonist, the American ambulance driver Frederic Henry, came from, or why he enlisted in the Italian army to begin with. (For that matter, we read chapter after chapter before even learning his name.) Nor do we discover much about his lover Catherine Barkley's past, other than the fact that her fiancé was killed in battle, in France.

There are no subplots, and the minor characters in *A Farewell to Arms* are minor indeed—for the simple fact that they are not needed. The power of this perennially popular book comes from the intensity of Frederic and Catherine's love for one another and from the power of the antagonistic forces that ultimately tear these two apart.

A Farewell to Arms is set against the historical and geographical background of World War I. Thus it contains numerous references to people and places, governments and fronts that Hemingway could safely assume his audience would recognize. In fact, certain basic information isn't alluded to in the book at all, as it was once common knowledge. (The book was published in 1929, only eleven years after the armistice of November 11, 1918, that ended the war.) For a contemporary audience, however, making sense of these references can be difficult. The continuing popularity of *A Farewell to Arms* attests to the fact that enjoyment of the novel does not depend upon understanding its particular setting. Here, however, are some basics:

World War I, or the Great War as it was then known, began in August 1914 with the assassination of the Austrian Archduke Francis Ferdinand. The war pitted the Central Powers (Germany and the Austro-Hungarian Empire) against the allied forces of Great Britain, France, Russia, and Italy, who were joined in 1917 by the United States. The action of *A Farewell to Arms* takes place from 1916–18 in four locations, for the most part: 1) the Julian Alps, along what was then the border between Italy and the Austro-Hungarian Empire; 2) the city of Milan, which lies in the plains of northern Italy, far from the front; 3) the Italian resort town of Stresa on Lake Maggiore, which straddles the border between Italy and Switzerland; and 4) various towns and villages of the Swiss Alps.

At the start of the book, the Italian army is busy keeping the Austro-Hungarian forces occupied so that the latter cannot assist the Germans on the war's western and eastern fronts. Later, Russia will withdraw due to the communist Revolution of 1917, and near the book's climax German troops will join the Austro-Hungarian forces, necessitating Italy's humiliating retreat from Caporetto. (This event, which the book's first readers would have recognized, provided the author with the opportunity for some of his most dramatic and effective writing ever.) Keep in mind as you read that Switzerland shares a border with Italy—and that Switzerland was neutral during World War I.

The context of *A Farewell to Arms* is not simply the First World War, however, but all the wars that preceded it, as well—or rather, the general notion of war as an opportunity for heroism. Hemingway writes here in the tradition of the greatest war stories ever told: Homer's *Iliad* and *War and Peace* by Leo Tolstoy. And certain techniques of Homer and Tolstoy (for instance, juxtaposing what we might call a "wide-screen" view of battle with "close-ups") were put to extremely effective use in *A Farewell to Arms*, starting in the book's very first chapter.

But like *The Red Badge of Courage*, the famous novel of the Civil War written by Stephen Crane (one of Hemingway's favorite American authors), *A Farewell to Arms* also reacts *against* the *Iliad* and *War and Peace* and many lesser stories of battlefield bravery. It tries to tell the often-ugly truth about war—to honestly depict life during wartime rather than glorifying it. Thus this book contains not just deserters (Frederic Henry and Catherine Barkley themselves), but illness and injury and incompetent leadership; it contains profanity (or at least implies it) and prostitution at the front. Frederic Henry's injury is incurred not in valorous combat but while he is eating spaghetti. The retreat from Caporetto disintegrates into sheer anarchy.

A Farewell to Arms is probably the best novel written about World War I (with Erich Maria Remarque's *All Quiet on the Western Front* a strong runner-up), and it bears comparison to the best American books about World War II (Norman Mailer's *The Naked and the Dead* and *Catch-22* by Joseph Heller among them), Korea (James Salter's *The Hunters*), and Vietnam (*The Things They Carried*, by Tim O'Brien).

And yet, *A Farewell to Arms* is at the same time a tender love story—one of the most tender and affecting ever written. It has been compared to William Shakespeare's *Romeo and Juliet*, and the reference is an apt one. Both stories concern young lovers antagonized by their societies.

(In Shakespeare's play, the Montague-Capulet blood feud is the problem; in Hemingway's novel, the Great War is to blame.) Both stories seem to vibrate with a sickening sense of doom that only increases as the stories near their respective conclusions. And both end in heartbreaking tragedy. If not one of the greatest love stories ever told, *A Farewell to Arms* is certainly among the greatest of the twentieth century.

Actually, it is the very combination of love and war that makes this book so potent and memorable. Regarding the woman he loves, the hero of Hemingway's novel *For Whom the Bell Tolls* tells himself "You had better love her very hard, and make up in intensity what the relation will lack in duration and continuity." Frederic Henry of *A Farewell to Arms* could say the same thing of his affair with Catherine Barkley. Because they meet in a time and place in which every day could be their last together, Frederic and Catherine must wring every drop of intimacy and passion from their relationship. (Notice how soon Catherine begins to speak of love, and how soon—especially considering the conservative mores of the time in which the book is set—they sleep together.) The result is an affair—and a story—almost unbearable in its intensity.

A Farewell to Arms is certainly one of Hemingway's finest novels. In fact, some critics have called it his best. Though not as inventive—as extreme, really—in subject and style as *The Sun Also Rises* (published three years earlier), this book actually benefits from its comparatively conventional approach to storytelling; it seems more sincere, more heartfelt. (Of course, *The Sun Also Rises* is about World War I, too. It merely focuses on the war's tragic aftermath.)

And like William Faulkner's *Light in August*, *A Farewell to Arms* proves that its author was not merely a Modern master. He could also produce a big book in the grand tradition of the nineteenth century novel. In retrospect, it is no surprise that *A Farewell to Arms* is the book that made Ernest Hemingway famous. As Robert Penn Warren wrote in his Introduction to a later edition of the novel, "*A Farewell to Arms* more than justified the early enthusiasm of the connoisseurs of Hemingway and extended this reputation from them to the public at large."

A Farewell to Arms feels less propagandistic than Hemingway's other great war story, *For Whom the Bell Tolls*—which relies partly on flashback for its effect and also descends at times into the stylistic mannerism that marred the author's later work. *A Farewell to Arms* is vastly superior to the remaining Hemingway novels (*To Have and Have Not* and *Across the River and Into the Trees*, and the posthumously published *Islands in the Stream* and *The Garden of Eden*) as well as the novellas *The Torrents of Spring* and *The Old Man and the Sea*. In fact, the only other volume in the Hemingway *oeuvre* that stands up to a comparison with *A Farewell to Arms* is the writer's debut story collection, *In Our Time*. That book's postwar tales, "Soldier's Home" and "Big Two-Hearted River," can almost be read as sequels to *A Farewell to Arms*, or at least to the events that inspired the novel.

A Brief Synopsis

A Farewell to Arms begins in the Alps around the frontier between Italy and present-day Slovenia. Allied with Britain, France, and Russia against the Austro-Hungarian Empire and Germany, Italy is responsible for preventing the Austro-Hungarian forces from assisting the Germans on the war's western front, and Russia in the east. The novel's narrator and protagonist is eventually identified as Lieutenant Frederic Henry, an American who has volunteered for the Italian army because the United States has not yet entered the war. Henry supervises a group of Italian ambulance drivers.

After a wintertime leave spent touring the country, Lieutenant Henry returns to the captured town at the front where his unit lives. One evening his roommate, a surgeon and lieutenant in the Italian army named Rinaldi, introduces Henry to two British nurses: Catherine Barkley and her friend Helen Ferguson. Catherine and Henry talk of the war and of her fiancé, killed in combat the year before; clearly she has been traumatized by the experience. On his second visit to the British hospital, they kiss. When Henry again visits Catherine, she tells him that she loves him and asks whether he loves her. He responds that he does.

One night, Lieutenant Henry and his fellow ambulance-drivers settle into a dugout across the river from the enemy troops. While the drivers are eating, the Austrian bombardment wounds Henry in the leg and kills one of the other drivers. Henry is transported by train to an American hospital in Milan.

Catherine Barkley arrives at the hospital, to which she has been transferred. Once again, she and Lieutenant Henry declare their love for each other, after which they have sex in the hospital bed. Henry and Catherine spend the summer together while he recuperates from an operation on his leg, visiting restaurants around Milan in the evening and then spending nights together. At summer's end, however, Lieutenant Henry is ordered back to the front, and Catherine tells him she is three months pregnant. On their last evening together in Milan, Henry buys a pistol, and he and Catherine take a room in a hotel.

Soon after Lieutenant Henry's return to the front, the Austrians (now joined by German troops) bombard the Italian army and eventually break through the lines near the town of Caporetto. Henry and the other ambulance drivers retreat with the rest of the Italian forces in a long, slow-moving column of troops and vehicles. They pick up two Italian engineer-sergeants. Finally, the ambulances pull off the main road. When one of the vehicles becomes stuck in the mud, the two sergeants refuse to assist in the effort to dislodge it and disobey Lieutenant Henry's order to remain with the group. He fires at them, wounding one; another ambulance driver then uses Henry's pistol to finish the job. Henry and the three drivers abandon the ambulances and set out on foot for the Tagliamento River, across which lies safety.

Soon they spot German soldiers in the distance. One driver is shot to death by fellow Italians firing in error. Another driver flees, to surrender to the Germans. Finally safe from the enemy, Lieutenant Henry observes that Italian army officers like himself are being shot by the military police for deserting their troops. He also fears being mistaken for a German spy. And so he dives into the Tagliamento River, deserting the Italian army, and swims ashore downstream. Henry crosses part of the Venetian plain on foot, then boards a moving train, hiding among guns stored beneath a tarpaulin.

Frederic (no longer Lieutenant) Henry arrives in Milan, incognito. Catherine Barkley and Helen Ferguson are absent from the hospital, having gone on holiday to the Italian resort town of Stresa. So Henry travels via train to Stresa, where he finds Catherine and Helen. Discovering late one night that Henry will be arrested as a deserter in the morning, Henry and Catherine quickly prepare to escape into neutral Switzerland. Through the stormy night, they travel in a small, open boat across Lake Maggiore. The following day they are arrested and briefly detained by Swiss officials, after which they are released.

Frederic Henry and Catherine Barkley move into a chalet on a mountain above Montreaux and spend an idyllic winter there. At winter's end, they leave the mountains for a hotel in Lausanne. Finally, Henry takes Catherine to the hospital, where her baby is stillborn. Then, as a result of multiple hemorrhages, Catherine dies as well.

List of Characters

Frederic Henry An American second-lieutenant in the ambulance corps of the Italian army during World War I.

Catherine Barkley A British nurse who falls in love with Henry following the death of her fiancé in battle.

The Priest The chaplain in Henry's unit. Baited by the other officers, he is befriended by Henry, to whom he offers spiritual advice.

Rinaldi Henry's roommate and friend, an Italian lieutenant and surgeon.

Helen Ferguson Catherine's friend and fellow nurse.

Passini and Bonello Ambulance drivers serving under Henry.

Manera, Gavuzzi, Gordini, Piani, and Aymo Other ambulance drivers.

Mrs. Walker An American nurse at the hospital in Milan.

Miss Gage Another American nurse, sympathetic to Henry and Catherine's affair.

Miss Van Campen The hostile superintendent of nurses.

Dr. Valentini A highly competent Italian surgeon, full of *joie de vivre*.

Meyers A somewhat sinister American expatriate.

Ettore Moretti An Italian-American from San Francisco serving with distinction in the Italian army.

Ralph Simmons An American student of opera and a friend to Henry.

Count Greffi An aging but vigorous Italian who befriends Henry in Stresa and serves as a mentor to him.

Character Map

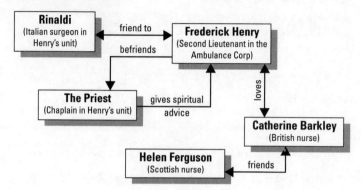

CRITICAL COMMENTARIES

Book One
Chapter I

Summary

Chapter I introduces the general setting of *A Farewell to Arms*: wartime during the early twentieth century (note the references to "motor trucks" and "motor cars"), in an agricultural region of an as-yet-unnamed country. The narrator, also unidentified so far, tells of fighting in the mountains beyond the plain where the action of the chapter takes place, mentioning that "things went very badly" for his side.

Commentary

The first chapter is short, but it could hardly be more significant, as it is here that Hemingway sets the tone for the entire novel to follow. This is to be a story of war, but one that tells the harsh truth about war rather than glorifying the topic: War is not picturesque and glamorous but rather dull and dangerous in equal measure.

Literary Device

Thus death and dying take center stage in the opening pages of *A Farewell to Arms*. Although these pages are set in a plain "rich with crops," rain will serve as a symbol of death in this novel. And so our narrator reports that "in the fall when the rains came the leaves all fell from the chestnut trees and the branches were bare and the trunks black with rain. The vineyards were thin and bare-branched too and all the country wet and brown and dead with autumn." The narrator also tells us that the rain was followed by disease. Thus Hemingway makes an explicit, even causal, connection between rain and death. He then foreshadows the novel's tragic conclusion when the soldiers weighed down by weapons and ammunition are said to march "as though they were six months gone with child."

Character Insight

Notice how the war moves past the narrator while he remains stationary, an observer of marching troops, mules, and trucks transporting weapons and supplies, and finally cars carrying officers as high-ranking as generals—even the King himself. Although we don't yet know the circumstances of the narrator's involvement in the conflict, we can tell that he is less than fully engaged in this war. (Later, we will learn that he is Frederic Henry, an American volunteer in the ambulance corps and a second lieutenant in the Italian army.) He is on its periphery, literally and perhaps philosophically as well.

A fundamental dichotomy of the novel is introduced in Chapter I: the tension between mountains and plains, highlands and lowlands. (Hemingway biographer Carlos Baker was one of the first commentators to stress this pattern in *A Farewell to Arms*.) In general during this story, activities that are disciplined and pure and therefore admirable tend to occur in the mountains, while the lowlands are the province of the weak, the corrupt.

Style & Language

Chapter I also raises the curtain on the distinctive and influential Hemingway style of writing, often summed up as the use of short, declarative sentences rich with specific, concrete detail. Just as typical of the writer's style, and even more distinctive, are long, compound sentences comprising short clauses in series—in effect, a chain of sentences linked by conjunctions (short, connective words like "and," "or," and "but"). For instance, "The trunks of the trees too were dusty and the leaves fell early that year and we saw the troops marching along the road and the dust rising and leaves, stirred by the breeze, falling and the soldiers marching and afterward the road bare and white except for the leaves."

Character Insight

Finally, we get a sense from this chapter of the narrator's attitude toward the unpleasant and difficult, the painful and even tragic. Regarding the cholera outbreak, he tells us that "in the end only seven thousand died of it in the army." *Only* seven thousand! Like all of Hemingway's heroes, the narrator *of A Farewell to Arms* is a stoic, understating rather than exaggerating, and grimly accepting what he cannot change.

Glossary

> (Here and in the following chapters, difficult words and phrases, as well as allusions and historical references, are explained.)

camion a motor truck or heavy dray wagon.

the King here, meaning Victor Emmanuel III (d. 1947), King of Italy (1900–46).

Udine a commune (that is, the smallest administrative district of local government) between the Tagliamento and Isonzo Rivers in the Venetia region of northeast Italy.

cholera any of various intestinal diseases; specifically, an acute, severe, infectious disease (Asiatic cholera) common in Asia, caused by bacteria and characterized by profuse diarrhea, intestinal pain, and dehydration.

Chapter II

Summary

A year passes, one in which there were "many victories." As a result, the side of the narrator (still identified only as "we") advances across a river and occupies a captured enemy town, Gorizia.

Evidently it is World War I, and the action in this chapter takes place in the Alps around the frontier between Italy and present-day Slovenia. Allied with Britain, France, and Russia against the Austro-Hungarian Empire and Germany, Italy is responsible for preventing the Austro-Hungarian forces from assisting the Germans in their fight against Britain and France on the war's western front, and Russia in the east.

Now Hemingway begins to introduce his cast of characters. During dinner in the officers' mess, on the night of winter's first snowfall, the narrator's fellow officers taunt the priest, their chaplain—though, significantly, the narrator himself does not join in the baiting. The Italian officers recommend that the narrator spend his forthcoming leave in a variety of low-lying Italian towns and cities, while the priest suggests he travel to the mountains.

Commentary

Literary Device

In this chapter, the writer introduces another dichotomy paralleling that of the mountains versus the plains: the church and the brothel. The two dynamics intersect when the priest invites the narrator to visit his mountain hometown while on leave. The officers scoff at this suggestion: "He doesn't want to see peasants," one says. "Let him go to centres of culture and civilization." Another officer then offers the addresses of whorehouses in Naples. To these men, civilization and sex are one and the same, but the priest is offering the narrator a different, more spiritual, way of living.

It was a fact of pre- and early-modern warfare that fighting became impossible when it snowed. Therefore snow equals peace to Henry and his compatriots, as it will late in the novel—although that peace is never more than temporary. Here snow covers the bare ground and even the artillery, but the stumps of the oak trees torn up by the summer's fighting continue to protrude from the blanket of white. Thus snow is merely a reprieve, a cease-fire.

Glossary

Gorizia a town in present-day northeast Italy, on the Isonzo River. At the time during which the story takes place, it lay within the boundaries of Austria-Hungary.

wistaria a twining woody vine or shrub of the pea family, with fruits that are pods and showy clusters of bluish, white, pink or purplish flowers.

bawdy house a house of prostitution.

Asti a wine from the city of the same name in the Piedmont region of northwest Italy.

mess a group of people who regularly have their meals together.

spaghetti course Sometimes called the primo piatto, or first course, it follows the antipasto in a traditional Italian meal and precedes the secundo piatto, or entrée.

tannic tasting of tannins absorbed from grape skins and seeds and from oak barrels; somewhat bitter or astringent.

five against one (slang) masturbating.

pidgin a mixed language, or jargon, incorporating the vocabulary of one or more languages with a very simplified form of the grammatical system of one of these and not used as the main language of any of its speakers.

Pope Pope Benedict XV (d. 1922), pope from 1914–22.

Franz Joseph (d. 1916) emperor of Austria (1848–1916) and king of Hungary (1867–1916).

Free Mason a member of an international secret society having as its principles brotherliness, charity, and mutual aid.

Amalfi a town in south Italy, on the Gulf of Salerno.

Palermo a seaport and the capital of Sicily, on the north coast.

Capri an island near the entrance to the Bay of Naples.

Abruzzi a region of central Italy, on the Adriatic Sea.

Capracotta a village in the Abruzzi region.

sotto-tenente (Italian) second lieutenant.

tenente (Italian) lieutenant.

capitano (Italian) captain.

maggiore (Italian) major.

tenente-colonello (Italian) lieutenant-colonel.

Caruso (1873–1921) Enrico, world-famous Italian operatic tenor.

Chapter III

Summary

In springtime, the narrator returns to Gorizia. His roommate and friend, a surgeon and lieutenant in the Italian army named Rinaldi, is introduced. Rinaldi asks the narrator about his leave and reports on the presence in the occupied town of what he calls "beautiful English girls," particularly a Miss Barkley. At the officers' mess in the evening, the narrator apologizes to the priest for not visiting the latter's home region of Abruzzi. Instead he spent his leave drinking and consorting with prostitutes. The baiting of the priest by his fellow Italian officers resumes.

Commentary

Upon the narrator's return to the front, what he earlier referred to as the "permanent rain" of winter is over for the time being, and in its place are warm sunshine and spring greenery. The absence here of the novel's primary symbol of death would seem to bode well. And yet the snow, the only thing that truly halts the fighting each year, has melted. Battle is therefore inevitable: "Next week the war starts again," Lieutenant Rinaldi reports.

Rinaldi is a humanist whose sensual values will be contrasted with the spiritual values of the priest. Rinaldi's relationship with the narrator is warm and easy and of a piece with Hemingway's treatment of male friendship in other books and stories. Miss Barkley, who will prove to be the heroine of *A Farewell to Arms*, is introduced almost as an aside. This is consistent with Hemingway's valuing of understatement, and it is also a realistic touch, as we often meet the most important people in our lives without great fanfare, even by accident.

Literary Device

The narrator's talk with the priest reiterates the mountains-plains dichotomy. Our narrator knows he should have traveled to Abruzzi, a "place where the roads were frozen and hard as iron, where it was clear and cold and dry and the snow was dry and powdery and hare-tracks in the snow and the peasants took off their hats and called you Lord and there was good hunting." Instead he has visited bars and whorehouses in the cities of the lowlands. For now, the narrator's strategy vis-à-vis the war specifically and the unpleasantness of the world in general could be referred to as obliteration, which he achieves via alcohol and sex. He is spiritually lost for the time being, and much of *A Farewell to Arms* will trace his movement toward self-realization.

Style & Language

As stated earlier, part of what makes the Hemingway style distinctive is its reliance on the actual rather than the theoretical. Note the specificity of the narrator's description of the room he shares with Rinaldi. Rather than telling us that this room is pleasantly familiar and yet slightly menacing, he focuses on the concrete: "The window was open," he reports, "my bed was made up with blankets and my things hung from the wall." The narrator lists these things (gas mask, helmet), then mentions his trunk, his boots, and his rifle. Without generalizing at all, Hemingway has told us much about the Spartan life of a soldier.

The Hemingway style reappears in the narrator's hallucinatory description of his winter leave: "I had gone to no such place," he says of Abruzzi, "but to the smoke of cafes and nights when the room whirled and you needed to look at the wall to make it stop, nights in bed, drunk, when you knew that that was all there was, and the strange excitement of waking and not knowing who it was with you, and the world all unreal in the dark and so exciting that you must resume again unknowing and not caring in the night, sure that this was all and all and all and not caring."

Again, in contrast to the received wisdom about Hemingway's style, this is not a short, declarative sentence; it is a long one that shows the influence of two writers Hemingway knew in Paris during the years before he wrote *A Farewell to Arms*. The technique known as *stream-of-consciousness*, an attempt to imitate the often illogical workings of the human mind, comes from the Irish writer James Joyce. Hemingway's teacher Gertrude Stein is probably responsible for his use of multiple conjunctions as well as repetition in general. (Stein's most famous sentences: "A rose is a rose is a rose," and "When you get there, there's no there there.")

Glossary

schutzen (German) marksmen.

Ciaou (Italian) Hello.

Villa San Giovanni, Messina, Taormina various locales in Italy.

the Cova restaurant in Milan.

Strega an after-dinner drink.

Chapter IV

Summary

Finally we learn about the particular nature of the narrator's involvement in the war: He supervises a group of ambulance drivers. At the start of this chapter, he briefly discusses the condition of the cars with his men. Rinaldi convinces the narrator to join him in visiting Miss Barkley. And so at sunset, on the grounds of a German villa converted to a British hospital, the narrator meets two nurses: Miss Barkley and her friend Helen Ferguson. Miss Barkley and the narrator talk of the war and of her fiancé, killed in combat the year before.

Commentary

Chapter IV is a key chapter both dramatically and thematically. In terms of the novel's action, it is when the protagonist of *A Farewell to Arms* meets the novel's heroine, setting the story proper in motion. Notice how quickly they become intimate; Catherine Barkley talks of her recent loss of the man to whom she was engaged, and the narrator admits that he has never loved anyone. Hemingway understands how rapidly people grow close during times of extraordinary stress.

Thematically, the narrator is already preparing for—that is, rationalizing—what will be the climactic act of the novel: his desertion from the Italian army. He does so here by telling himself and us that his leave has not affected the smooth and successful operation of his unit: "It evidently made no difference whether I was there to look after things or not" and "The whole thing seemed to run better while I was away." In other words, if the narrator chooses to abandon his commitment to the cause someday, this will have no discernible negative effect on the war. Along these lines, Miss Barkley's observation, "What an odd thing—to be in the Italian army," is significant, the first of many such remarks that will give the narrator a kind of permission, ultimately, to desert. After all, he joined voluntarily, and it is not even his own country he is fighting for.

Theme

Notice also how Rinaldi and the narrator pause for not one but two drinks of grappa before going to meet Miss Barkley and Miss Ferguson. One of the themes that runs throughout Hemingway's work, including *A Farewell to Arms*, is that encounters between the sexes can be just as terrifying (and just as dangerous—this one will result in two deaths) as battlefield combat. Thus it is necessary to fortify oneself for such meetings.

Finally, it is typical of Hemingway not to provide much in the way of physical descriptions of his characters. Miss Barkley, for instance, "was quite tall. She wore what seemed to me to be a nurse's uniform, was blonde and had a tawny skin and gray eyes. I thought she was very beautiful." Hemingway realized that this lack of specifics would accomplish two things: 1) allow his readers to fill in the blanks with their own details, making them active participants in the storytelling experience, and 2) lend a sense of universality to his characters. In a sense, anyone could be the hero or the heroine of *A Farewell to Arms*.

Glossary

battery an emplacement for heavy guns, or a fortification equipped with such guns.

Signor Tenente (Italian) Mr. Lieutenant.

on permission on leave.

gasoline park a station for refueling motor vehicles.

infantry that branch of an army consisting of soldiers equipped and trained to fight chiefly on foot.

Hugo's English grammar an English-language textbook.

Grappa an Italian brandy distilled from the lees left after pressing grapes to make wine.

the Somme a river in north France, site of brutal fighting between Allied and German forces during World War I.

sabre a heavy cavalry sword with a slightly curved blade. Swords were rendered largely ineffectual by the development of firearms, thus Catherine's reference is ironic.

abbastanza bene (Italian) rather well.

pas encore (French) not really.

Chapter V

Summary

The narrator calls on Miss Barkley and is told by the head nurse at the hospital that she is on duty. He examines the preparations being made for the planned Italian offensive against the Austrians, and while he reconnoiters the area, four Austrian shells explode nearby. After dinner the narrator visits Miss Barkley again, and they kiss.

Commentary

After what seems like token resistance on her part, the affair between the narrator and Miss Barkley begins. Clearly they have different agendas, however. The narrator sees their relationship as a chess game. By contrast, Miss Barkley seems to be projecting her love for her lost fiancé onto the narrator: She cries when they kiss for the first time, begs him to be good to her, and tells him rather enigmatically that "we're going to have a strange life."

Literary Device

The foreshadowing of the narrator's desertion continues in his discussion with the head nurse, who also finds it odd that he enlisted with the Italians. He himself feels uncomfortable giving the Italian salute. During his talk with Miss Barkley, the narrator suggests "Let's drop the war." Her response: "It's very hard. There's no place to drop it." After she slaps him following an attempted kiss, he jokes, "And we have gotten away from the war." She laughs. At this point in the story, Miss Barkley already knows that the war can't simply be "dropped." As the tragic loss of a loved one has taught her, the war has consequences. The narrator, however, is not yet aware of this fact.

Glossary

rivederci, a rivederla (Italian) until we meet again; goodbye: implies temporary parting.

Plava town on the Isonzo River, in present-day Slovenia.

trench a long, narrow ditch dug by soldiers for cover and conceal-ment, with the removed earth heaped up in front. Protracted trench warfare was characteristic of World War I, especially on the Western Front, in France.

pontoon bridge a temporary bridge supported by flat-bottom boats, or some other floating objects, such as hollow cylinders.

dugout a shelter, as in warfare, dug in the ground or in a hillside.

dressing station a temporary hospital.

grade the degree of rise or descent of a sloping surface.

carabinieri (Italian) military police.

seventy-sevens shells fired by the Austrians.

V.A.D. Volunteer Air Detachment.

cloistered secluded or confined as in a cloister (a monastery or convent).

Chapter VI

Summary

After three days, the narrator again visits Miss Barkley, whose first name the writer reveals here to be Catherine. They sit in the garden beside the British hospital and talk: She asks him for reassurance that he loves her, which he provides. Then Catherine speaks of her own love for him. Later, she refers sadly to the exchange as a game, and after kissing they part for the evening.

Commentary

In terms of the plot, an object that will prove significant later in the novel is introduced in Chapter VI: the pistol that the narrator is required to wear. We are constantly reminded of the nearness of war in these relatively peaceful chapters by the presence of such "props."

Meanwhile, Catherine Barkley coaxes a declaration of love from the narrator, though he tells us that it is a lie. "I did not love Catherine Barkley nor had any idea of loving her," he elaborates, comparing their affair to a game again (bridge, this time). Soon, however, the tables are turned. Catherine will not let the narrator put his arm around her, resists his kisses, and reveals that she knows he has been playing a game. She is playing one too: "You don't have to pretend you love me," she tells the narrator. "You see I'm not mad . . . ." Again, Catherine proves wiser than she at first appeared—wiser in the ways of the world, so far, than the narrator himself.

Another typical Hemingway touch ends the chapter. Often the writer lets us know how his characters are feeling not by reading their minds, describing their actions, or even quoting their dialogue, but by offering the reader the reactions that these characters inspire in others. Though he never says so explicitly, we know that the narrator is agitated after his visit with Nurse Barkley because of his roommate's response to his behavior: "Ah, ha! . . . It does not go so well," Rinaldi says. "Baby [that is, the narrator] is puzzled."

Glossary

frescoes a painting made with watercolors on wet plaster.

Chapter VII

Summary

While driving his ambulance, the narrator encounters a fellow American, an infantryman fighting with the Italians who wants to be excused from combat because of the pain caused by a hernia. The narrator concocts a scheme: The infantryman should intentionally injure himself in the head. The American does so. Later, while writing home from his quarters, the narrator muses about alternatives to his situation and fantasizes about sex with Catherine Barkley in a hotel room in Milan. In the officers' mess on his way to see Catherine, the narrator gets drunk (it is at this point in the narrative that we finally learn his name: Frederic Henry) while the officers once again torment the priest. As a result, Henry shows too late to see Catherine; he goes home feeling "lonely and hollow."

Commentary

Again Lieutenant Henry's desertion is foreshadowed, as he agrees with the soldier from Pittsburgh that they are engaged in a "rotten" war, then suggests (apparently without any guilt) a means by which the infantryman can opt out of the fighting. This episode is significant because it shows us that disillusionment with the war is not limited to Henry himself.

The narrator's name, incidentally, may allude to the protagonist of the American antiwar novel *The Red Badge of Courage*, whose war wound was as absurd as the Lieutenant's will be. Hemingway greatly admired that book's writer, Stephen Crane. The writer's refusal to reveal Henry's name until now is another strategy by which the protagonist's Everyman status is emphasized. It also stresses the faceless, interchangeable nature of soldiers in wartime; to those in charge, Hemingway seems to be saying, one ambulance driver is as good as any other, and all are merely bodies.

The naivete about the war exhibited by Henry in earlier scenes with Catherine Barkley is made explicit here: "Well, I knew I would not be killed," he thinks. "Not in this war. It did not have anything to do with

me. It seemed no more dangerous to me myself than war in the movies."
Again, Catherine knows that the war is very real as a result of having
lost her fiancé to the fighting, but Henry has had no such experience—
yet. She also knows what Henry will learn: His detachment and lack of
fear do not mean that the realities and dangers of the war do not exist
or that he is immune to them.

Once more, Henry does not participate in the tormenting of the
priest. He perhaps recognizes that the chaplain stands for something,
unlike the cynical, nihilistic officers who taunt him. Henry himself
doesn't believe in much of anything yet, but his refusal to join in the
ritual of priest-baiting shows us that he respects those who do and that
he has potential in this regard.

Stylistically, Hemingway combines the short, declarative sentences
for which he is best known with Joycean stream-of-consciousness in
Frederick's reverie about sharing a Milan hotel room with Catherine.
Note that although the emphasis seems to be on the sexual, Henry says
that "we would both love each other all night": an unconscious admis-
sion of his deepening feelings toward her. Still, he is uncommitted
enough at this point in the story that he can miss an evening with
Catherine altogether because he is drinking with his fellow officers.
On the other hand, he does regret doing so afterwards. Henry is growing, and growing closer to Catherine.

Glossary

smistimento (Italian) sorting or shunting place.

brigata (Italian) brigade.

spile a heavy stake or timber driven into the ground as a foundation
or support.

horse ambulance an ambulance drawn by horses.

hernia the protrusion of all or part of an organ through a tear in the
wall of the surrounding structure; especially, the protrusion of part
of the intestine through the abdominal muscles; a rupture.

Zona di Guerra (Italian) war zone.

Il Generale Cadorna Italian general.

Aosta the Valle d'Aosta, a region of northwest Italy.

Black Forest a wooded mountain region in southwest Germany.

Carpathians the Carpathian Mountains, a mountain system in central Europe, extending southeast from south Poland through the Czech Republic and Ukraine into northeast Romania.

Via Manzoni a street in Milan.

capri bianca an Italian white wine.

Archbishop Ireland American archbishop, apparently, with whose case Henry is unfamiliar.

Béziers a city in south France.

Bacchus the Roman god of wine and revelry; identified with the Greek Dionysus.

. . . Frederico Enrico or Enrico Federico? Bassi wants to know if the Lieutenant's name is Frederic Henry or Henry Frederic. (It is the former.)

cypress an evergreen, cone-bearing tree, with dark foliage and a distinctive symmetrical form.

Chapter VIII

Summary

Instructed to drive an ambulance to the river in preparation for a nocturnal attack there, Lieutenant Henry stops first at the British hospital, where Catherine Barkley gives him a Saint Anthony medal.

Commentary

This chapter does little besides set the stage for the dramatic action to follow in Chapter IX. In fact, Hemingway explicitly foreshadows that action, as Lieutenant Henry says of the St. Anthony medal, "After I was wounded I never found him."

As usual, the author underplays drama and avoids melodrama: Catherine and Henry don't even kiss while bidding one another goodbye—presumably a result of hospital decorum or her British reserve. And as in an earlier scene, we learn about Henry's feelings not from the narrator himself but via the reaction of another character: "No, you can't kiss me here," Catherine says.

Literary Device

In terms of the novel's symbolism, it is significant that Henry ascends from the lowlands into the hills for his first encounter with heroism. And it is interesting that he says of the white mountains in the distance that "Those were all the Austrians' mountains and we had nothing like them." Again, Henry seems to be constructing a rationale for his forthcoming abandonment from the Italian army, albeit unconsciously. Unlike the Austrians, he suggests, the Italians are undisciplined, and thus perhaps they are not quite worth fighting for.

Glossary

Cormons town west of Gorizia, in northeast Italy.

a Saint Anthony a St. Anthony medal. St. Anthony of Padua is the Roman Catholic patron saint of miracles. He is also a patron saint of Italy.

convoy a group of vehicles traveling together for mutual protection or convenience.

fez a brimless felt hat shaped like a truncated cone, usually red, with a flat crown from which a long, black tassel hangs: the Turkish national headdress of men in the nineteenth and early twentieth centuries.

bersaglieri (Italian) riflemen.

Chapter IX

Summary

Lieutenant Henry and his fellow ambulance drivers establish themselves in a dugout across the river from the enemy troops. The drivers argue over the purpose of the war, with the driver named Passini the most philosophically opposed. While the drivers are eating, the Austrian bombardment wounds Henry and kills Passini, after which Henry is transported away from the fighting in great pain.

Commentary

Dramatically, this chapter provides the novel's second major turning point, as Lieutenant Henry's war wound will remove him from action and thus enable his affair with Catherine Barkley to grow into love.

Theme

Thematically, Hemingway uses the discussion among the drivers in the dugout to articulate his beliefs on war, or at least his beliefs on World War I. (The writer was an ardent supporter of the Republican, or anti-Fascist, side in the Spanish Civil War, subject of his later novel *For Whom the Bell Tolls*.) Since Henry is relatively inexperienced and therefore naïve at this point in the novel, it is Passini who puts these ideas into words: that nothing is worse than war, that war makes men go crazy, that those who fear their superiors are responsible for war. "Everybody hates this war," Passini says. Perhaps Passini plants the idea of a separate peace in Henry's head when he states, "One side must stop fighting. Why don't we stop fighting? If they come down into Italy they will get tired and go away."

Henry, by contrast, is still talking about bravery (though, significantly, he does admit after the first shelling to being scared). In a bit of foreshadowing that will prove ironic, he argues against giving up: "It would only be worse if we stopped fighting." He says defeat is worse than war itself.

The topic of desertion is explicitly addressed—specifically, the consequences of desertion from the Italian army. One of the drivers tells Henry that, when one unit wouldn't attack, military police shot every tenth man, and according to Passini, even the families of deserters are punished. Keep in mind how the writer has carefully planted the information about the brutality of the military polices; later, Hemingway's investment will pay off for writer and reader alike.

Consistent with the novel's first chapter, Chapter IX powerfully illustrates Hemingway's belief (at least during this stage of his life and career) that war is unglamorous. Notice that Henry is wounded and Passini killed not while performing daring feats of heroism, but while eating cold spaghetti. Henry's attempt to save Passini's life while he himself suffers is certainly heroic, but the scene is more absurd than epic.

In this chapter, Henry is finally exposed to the reality of the battlefield. As a result of his own intense pain and the trauma of witnessing the death of a comrade (not to mention the chapter's final scene, in which he is soaked by the blood of a dying soldier), Henry will no longer be able to deny his involvement in this war or its potential to affect him. The naivete that he displayed earlier in the book is evaporating, and Henry is beginning to approach the understanding of life and death that Catherine has possessed since they met.

Finally, notice how Hemingway continues to focus on the concrete and the specific, not only in his bravura description of the explosion that wounds Henry, but in small ways as well. When a shell hits nearby while Henry and Gordini are returning to the dugout with food, Henry tells us that "I was after him, holding the cheese, its smooth surface covered with brick dust." The detail of the brick dust on the cheese brings the scene alive.

Glossary

screens of corn-stalk and straw matting and matting over the top used here as camouflage.

observation balloons During World War I, military observers often ascended in balloons to observe the battle preparations of the enemy from aloft.

the war in Libya Libya was won by Italy from the Ottoman Empire in 1912.

wound-stripes insignie, like the American Purple Heart, indicating that the wearer has been wounded in battle.

Fiat radiator the nose of a car or truck made by the Italian automobile manufacturer.

mess tins portable metal plates, bowls, and cups, for eating on the march or on the battlefield.

granatieri (Italian) Grenadiers.

Grenadier a member of a special regiment or corps.

Alpini (Italian) Alpine troops.

V.E. soldiers troops fighting on the Italian side.

Evviva l'esercito (Italian) Long live the army.

San Gabriele town near the present-day border between Italy and Slovenia.

Monfalcone town in present-day northeast Italy, between the Isonzo River and the Gulf of Trieste. At the time during which the story takes place, it lay within the boundaries of Austria-Hungary.

Trieste seaport in present-day northeast Italy, on an inlet (Gulf of Trieste) of the Adriatic Sea. At the time during which the story takes place, it lay within the boundaries of Austria-Hungary.

cognac a French brandy distilled from wine in the area of Cognac, France.

Savoia region in southeast France, on the borders of Italy and Switzerland: a former duchy and part of the kingdom of Sardinia: annexed by France (1860).

pasta asciutta (Italian) dry pasta.

four hundred twenty a 420-millimeter mortar.

minnenwerfer (German) literally, "mine-thrower."

big Skoda guns a type of artillery.

three hundred fives 305-millimeter guns.

mama mia (Italian) my mother.

Dio te salve, Maria (Italian) God hail you, Mary.

Porta feriti! (Italian) Take the wounded!

tourniquet any device for compressing a blood vessel to stop bleeding or control the circulation of blood to some part, as a bandage twisted about a limb and released at intervals.

puttees coverings for the lower leg, in the form of a cloth or leather gaiter, or cloth strips wound spirally.

wallahs persons connected with a particular thing or function.

He is the legitimate son of President Wilson The doctor is trying to encourage special attention for Lieutenant Henry.

Ça va bien? (French) Are you doing well?

Antitetanus inoculation against tetanus, an acute infectious disease, often fatal, caused by the specific toxin of a bacillus which usually enters the body through wounds: it is characterized by spasmodic contractions and rigidity of some or all of the voluntary muscles, especially of the jaw, face, and neck.

I'll paint all this The doctor is offering to swab Lieutenant Henry's wounds with antiseptic.

Vive la France (French) Long live France.

sergeant-adjutant a staff officer who serves as an administrative assistant to the commanding officer.

Chapter X

Summary

Rinaldi visits Lieutenant Henry in the field hospital, reporting that the battle was won by the Italians. Rinaldi also says he will send Catherine Barkley to visit.

Commentary

This chapter dramatizes Lieutenant Henry's physical discomfort, post-wound, as well as emphasizing the warm friendship he shares with Rinaldi. Typically, the Hemingway hero is a modest man as well as a stoic. Here, despite prodding from Rinaldi ("You must have done something heroic either before or after."), Henry keeps mum about his genuinely admirable effort to save Passini.

Style & Language

Stylistically, Chapter X consists almost entirely of dialogue, and "untagged" dialogue at that. (That is, it lacks "he said" for the most part.) This is a technique that Hemingway developed in earlier short stories, especially "Hills Like White Elephants" from the 1927 collection *Men Without Women*. Notice that even when Hemingway does attribute dialogue, he does so as simply as possible, with "said" or "asked" rather than elaborate synonyms of these words.

Glossary

Medaglia d'argento (Italian) silver medal.

coup de main a surprise attack or movement, as in war.

The Lancet medical journal.

get excited become sexually aroused.

dago (slang) a person, often dark-skinned, of Spanish, Portuguese, or Italian descent: a term of hostility and contempt.

wop (slang) an Italian or a person of Italian descent: an offensive term of hostility and contempt.

Chapter XI

Summary

The priest visits Lieutenant Henry in the field hospital. They discuss the priest's alienation from their military unit and his dislike for the war, as well as Henry's lack of traditional religious beliefs.

Commentary

"It made me feel very young to have the dark come after the dusk and then remain. It was like being put to bed after supper," Lieutenant Henry tells us. Remarkably, we still know almost nothing about his childhood and adolescence, or precisely how and why he became involved in the war. (We will never discover much about either.)

In general, Hemingway struggled to tell effective stories with as little of this sort of background (sometimes called *exposition*) as possible. Here he especially wanted to avoid complicating his tale with the issue of his protagonist's motivation, because any hint of altruism on Henry's part would imply just the sort of ethical code that he lacks before meeting Catherine. Moreover, if war is like life, as Hemingway seems to argue here, then we don't have a choice in the matter of our involvement. For both of these reasons, the author wants us to focus on the here and now of the story, not the whys and wherefores.

Theme

The priest tells Henry that he hates the war and reiterates the theme introduced by Passini that the war is made by certain people and executed by others. Henry still resists this notion. He also admits that he does not love God—that perhaps he does not love anyone. "You will," the priest reassures him. "I know you will." Clearly the priest knows Lieutenant Henry better than Henry knows himself. After the priest departs, Henry muses about the pure life in the priest's home region of Abruzzi, thus reintroducing the mountains-lowlands dichotomy.

Note the particular nature of the contrast between the peace-loving priest and Rinaldi, who is warm and likeable but attracted by the violence and sex associated with wartime. At this point in *A Farewell to*

Arms, Henry stands somewhere between them, philosophically, as if at a crossroads. It is unclear whose path he will follow, despite his traumatic and painful recent experience.

Glossary

vermouth a sweet or dry, white fortified wine flavored with aromatic herbs, used in cocktails and as an aperitif.

The News of the World a British tabloid newspaper.

Mestre a town in northeast Italy, just northwest of Venice.

Gran Sasso D'Italia literally, "Great Stone of Italy."

Aquila town in the Abruzzi region of Italy.

Chapter XII

Summary

Rinaldi and the major from the mess visit Lieutenant Henry in the field hospital on the night before Henry is to be transferred to an American-run hospital in Milan for special treatment. They drink brandy together, and Rinaldi delivers the news that Catherine Barkley will be at that hospital. Henry departs for Milan by train.

Commentary

Another turning point in the narrative: Lieutenant Henry and Catherine Barkley are sent to the same hospital. But first Hemingway reminds us of the gravity of the general situation, as Henry speaks of patients dying in his ward and of those buried in the garden outside.

Stylistically, the author combines direct and indirect discourse with stream-of-consciousness in the long paragraphs describing the drunken visit by Rinaldi and the major. That is, the author quotes directly from their conversation rather than summarizing, but he disposes with the convention of setting off individual speeches via quotation marks and paragraphs. It all flows together in an imitation of an intoxicated person's experience of the conversation.

Glossary

mechano-therapy the treatment of disease, injuries, etc. by using mechanical devices, massage, etc.

"They asked me if I would declare war on Turkey" Turkey became allied with the Central Powers (Germany and Austria-Hungary) after the start of World War I in 1914.

Bulgaria Bulgaria too became allied with the Central Powers after the start of the war.

"We will get Nice and Savoia from the French. We will get Corsica and all the Adriatic coast-line." The major is alluding to territories held at one time or another by Italian city-states but not currently in their possession.

"I will never forget Romulus suckling the Tiber." According to legend, Romulus, founder of Rome, was said to have been suckled by a she-wolf. The Tiber is the river on which Rome was built. This is nonsensical, drunken talk.

to the Crystal Palace, to the Cova, to Campari's, to Biffi's, to the galleria . . . the Gran Italia . . . the Scala Sites of interest around Milan. The galleria is the Victor Emmanuel Gallery, a glass-covered walkway lined with shops. La Scala is Milan's world-famous opera house.

sight draft a means of wiring money overseas.

Garibaldi Giuseppe (1807–82); Italian patriot and general: leader in the movement to unify Italy.

riparto (Italian) division.

Vicenza commune in north Italy.

Book Two
Chapter XIII

Summary

Arriving in Milan, Lieutenant Henry is taken by ambulance to the American hospital, which proves empty except for two nurses, neither of whom is Catherine Barkley.

Commentary

In this chapter, Hemingway briefly reiterates the theme of Lieutenant Henry's alienation from the war, further preparing him and us for his eventual flight from involvement. He is the first and only patient in the American hospital, which barely functions as it lacks a doctor. Mainly the author is setting the stage here for the escalation of Henry's affair with Catherine Barkley; the American hospital in Milan will serve as a kind of refuge for them and their love, until Henry is sent back to the front at the conclusion of Book Two.

Notice, at chapter's end, Henry's inability to sleep well at night. Throughout his hospital stay, he will continue to sleep mainly during the daytime. Hemingway's heroes are often afraid of the dark.

Glossary

armoire a large, usually ornate cupboard or clothespress.

Lake Como lake in Lombardy, north Italy.

the Isonze the Isonzo River, in northeast Italy. At the time during which the story takes place, it lay within the boundaries of Austria-Hungary.

Cinzano brand-name of an aperitif.

fiasco (Italian) flask.

chianti a dry red wine produced in the Tuscany region of Italy.

eggnog a thick drink made of beaten eggs, milk, sugar, and nutmeg, often containing whiskey, rum, wine, etc.

sherry a Spanish fortified wine varying in color from light yellow to dark brown and in flavor from very dry to sweet.

Chapter XIV

Summary

A strangely hostile barber shaves Lieutenant Henry. Afterward, Henry discovers that the barber thought he was Austrian rather than American. Catherine Barkley arrives. She and Henry declare their love for one another and have sex in the hospital bed.

Commentary

The barber scene provides comic relief, but it also reiterates the theme of alienation; Lieutenant Henry is not recognized as an ally by the very Italians in whose army he serves.

When Henry and Catherine Barkley reunite, he declares his love for her, which might merely be his means of seducing her. But he tells us as well: "When I saw her I was in love with her. Everything turned over inside of me." And, at chapter's end, "God knows I had not wanted to fall in love with her. I had not wanted to fall in love with anyone. But God knows I had . . . "

Character Insight

For Henry, his affair with Catherine is no longer a game, and it is significant that this transformation follows his wounding in battle. The experience has matured Henry, elevating him to a level of wisdom closer to that of Catherine. Recall the way in which Hemingway implicitly connected love and war in Chapter IV by showing Henry and Rinaldi sharing a drink before their visit with the nurses, just as the soldiers drink before going into combat. Now combat has prepared Henry for love.

Glossary

lira the basic monetary unit of Italy.

signorino (Italian) young master.

Chapter XV

Summary

After three doctors together examine Lieutenant Henry's wound and x-rays, they recommend he wait six months before an operation on his leg. Henry seeks a second opinion, and an Italian major named Dr. Valenti proposes operating the following day.

Commentary

In this chapter, Hemingway dramatizes the contrast between the bureaucratic and the active—similar to that between those who made the war and those who actually fight it. (Nurse Van Campen and Nurse Gage embody this contrast as well.) The three doctors who first examine Lieutenant Henry are clearly incompetent as well as indecisive. Henry tells us that "doctors who fail in the practice of medicine have a tendency to seek one another's company and aid in consultation . . . These were three such doctors." Dr. Valenti, on the other hand, is full of *joie de vivre*: Henry says that he "laughed all the time" and even agrees to share a drink with Henry, for instance. In some ways, he seems more English than Italian and thus more of a kindred spirit to Henry; Dr. Valenti appreciates Catherine's beauty and says "Cheery oh." Again, the circumstances (incompetent doctors, lack of availability of "other opinions," and so on), not the individual, determine the care that Henry gets. In real life, it is not likely that Dr. Valenti would appear, and Hemingway knew it.

Literary Device

Chapter XV all but overflows with foreshadowing: In the very first paragraph, Henry tells us that the doctor "used a local anaesthetic called something or other 'snow.'" Recall that snow is all that forestalls combat in this war, and bear the symbolism of snow in mind during the last third of *A Farewell to Arms*, when it provides another kind of reprieve. Also remember Dr. Valenti's offer, "I will do all your maternity work free . . . She will make you a fine boy," he says of Catherine.

Glossary

Ospedale Maggiore (Italian) Great Hospital.

articulation a joint between bones.

synovial fluid the clear albuminous lubricating fluid secreted by the membranes of joint cavities, tendon sheaths, etc.

Cheery oh Dr. Valentini is trying to ingratiate himself with Catherine through the use of the British expression "cheerio." Hemingway's spelling indicates that his pronunciation isn't quite idiomatic.

Chapter XVI

Summary

Lieutenant Henry and Catherine Barkley spend the night before his operation together, in his hospital room.

Commentary

Style & Language

Hemingway reminds us that this otherwise peaceful chapter takes place during wartime with allusions to searchlights and the anti-aircraft gun. He sets the stage as well with carefully chosen specifics: the smell of the dew outside, for instance, as well as that of the coffee drunk by the gunners on the roof adjacent to the hospital. Such intimate sense details put the reader "in" the scene itself.

Literary Device

The dynamic of Lieutenant Henry's naivete versus Catherine Barkley's experience and maturity is reiterated as Henry tries to make a date for the night after the operation, and she insists he will be in no shape to see her. And the novel's ending is foreshadowed in the couple's playful exchange regarding their children's temperatures and in Catherine's insistence that Henry recuperate so they can go somewhere together: "Maybe the war will be over," she says hopefully. "It can't always go on."

Finally, a discussion of Henry's experience with prostitutes illustrates the difference between sex and true love. He tells Catherine that he has never loved anyone before her but admits to the reader that he is lying to her when he says he's never professed love to a partner. During this scene, the morning sun illuminates the spires of the Milan cathedral, perhaps reminding us of the priest. "I was clean inside and outside and waiting for the doctor," Henry tells us in the next sentence, allying himself with the chaplain rather than Rinaldi and the other officers—at least for the time being.

Style &
Language

Stylistically, Chapter XVI consists almost entirely of untagged dialogue. Notice how the content of the quotes as well as their diction (word choice) and syntax (sentence structure) makes attribution for the most part unnecessary. Catherine often addresses Henry as "darling," and her speeches tend to be longer and more overtly emotional than his.

Glossary

the cathedral Milan's famous cathedral, designed and built in the Gothic style. It is the second-largest church in Italy, after St. Peter's Basilica in Rome.

Chapter XVII

Summary

Chapter XVII summarizes the routine that Lieutenant Henry and Catherine Barkley fall into after his operation. She volunteers for night duty so as to spend time with him, and he sleeps during the day. Catherine's friend Helen Ferguson speaks cynically about love and suggests that Henry encourage Catherine to take time off from working nights so as to get some rest herself.

Commentary

Literary Device

This chapter, from which Catherine Barkley is mainly absent, is full nevertheless of ominous foreshadowing in the discussion between Lieutenant Henry and Helen Ferguson. Henry asks Nurse Ferguson if she'll attend his wedding to Catherine. Nurse Ferguson insists they will never be married; instead, she says, they'll "fight . . . . Fight or die." Crying, she continues, "But watch out you don't get her in trouble [that is, pregnant]. You get her in trouble and I'll kill you." Henry promises not to. Helen responds, "I don't want her with any of these war babies."

Theme

In this exchange, Hemingway draws a continuum, a straight line that runs from the kind of fighting that goes on between combatants in war, to sex and marriage, to fighting between couples (often referred to as the Battle of the Sexes), to childbirth, and back again. Though love and war seem to be exact opposites, the writer subtly suggests that they are, in fact, connected.

Also, Hemingway reiterates the theme of Henry's alienation from the Italian army by alluding to three other American soldiers staying in the hospital; one is there because he tried to dismantle an Austrian shell so as to take home a souvenir. The implication: the Americans involved on this front are dilettantes, neither truly serious about the cause nor entirely cognizant of war's consequences. Prior to receiving his wounds, this was certainly true of Henry himself.

Chapter XVIII

Summary

Lieutenant Henry and Catherine Barkley spend the summer together while he recuperates, visiting restaurants around Milan in the evening, and then spending nights together. They talk about marriage.

Commentary

As Lieutenant Henry grows more mobile, progressing from bed to carriage to crutches, his affair with Catherine Barkley develops into a full-blown idyll—despite the fact that it is summertime, the season of war. During one of the many nights they spend together, the couple discusses marriage, which Henry wants ("because I worried about having a child if I thought about it") but Catherine resists for practical reasons. It would necessitate their separation, she explains—more worldly in these matters than he, as usual. She reminds him of her experience being formally engaged, to the soldier who died. Like Nurse Ferguson in the prior chapter, Catherine intuits a not entirely logical connection between love and death.

Thematically, we return to the dynamic first dramatized near the start of the novel via the priest versus the officers, as Catherine tells Henry that she has no religion; she quickly corrects this statement, however, explaining "You're my religion." Catherine rejects organized faith, and yet she is no nihilist. She lives by a definite value system, and what she values is love.

Less able so far to reject traditional religion, Henry suggests a private or secret marriage of some kind, possibly an allusion by Hemingway to Shakespeare's *Romeo and Juliet* and therefore a premonition of tragedy. "I suppose all sorts of dreadful things will happen to us," Catherine says ominously, on the last page of the chapter. "But you don't have to worry about that." Again and again, Hemingway drops hints of catastrophe to come, filling us with foreboding.

Glossary

fresa, barbera   wines sampled by Henry and Catherine.

margaux   Chateau Margaux, a French wine.

Chapter XIX

Summary

Lieutenant Henry continues to recuperate, during a summer when "there were many victories in the papers"—at least on the Austrian front. Around Milan, he encounters an American couple, professional gamblers named Mr. and Mrs. Meyers; Ettore Moretti, an Italian from San Francisco who is a captain in the Italian army; and two American students of opera.

Commentary

Once again, Hemingway returns to the theme of Lieutenant Henry's alienation from the Italians in the midst of whom he lives and works, this time by comparing him to other Americans in Milan. According to rumor, Meyers lives in Italy after having been released from jail to die, and the two opera students have changed their American names to Italian ones, although one can't even pronounce the language properly. Ettore Moretti, the San Franciscan whose connection to Italy is most genuine (his parents live in Torino), is "a legitimate hero who bored everyone he met," according to Henry. None of these characters really belongs here—which again raises the question (or at least implies it), why is Henry himself in the Italian army? Once more, the writer is providing him with an excuse to desert later in the story.

With regard to characterization, note that while Henry tolerates Ettore Moretti, Catherine dislikes him intensely. Not only is she a more mature character than Henry at this point in the novel, she is also more developed as a Hemingway hero. (This would seem to refute the often-stated charge that the writer was a misogynist.) "We have heroes too," Catherine Barkley says of Moretti, "But usually, darling, they're much quieter." Catherine believes in the virtues of stoicism and modesty—virtues embodied not only in Henry (who will compare himself later to a middling baseball player) as well as Catherine, but in Hemingway's writing style, as well. (Ironically, though the writer himself may have been stoic, he was hardly modest; in fact, he is remembered as a true braggart.)

Literary
Device

Finally, it is in this chapter that the deeper meaning of the rain is made explicit. Catherine admits to Henry that "I'm afraid of the rain because sometimes I see myself dead in it . . . . And sometimes I see you dead in it." Thus Hemingway has combined symbolism and fore-shadowing in one image, and as we move forward through the story we will pay particular attention to the fortunes of the characters each time that it rains. To some degree, from this point on, we are reading *A Farewell to Arms* to discover whether or not Catherine dies. (Henry does not die, clearly, as he is the character telling the story.)

Glossary

Treatments . . . for bending the knees, mechanical treatments, baking in a box of mirrors with violet rays, massage, and baths examples of mechano-therapy mentioned in Chapter XII.

Kuk a mountain in present-day Slovenia.

Bainsizza plateau a plateau in present-day Slovenia.

Verona town in Veneto region of north Italy.

Hundred Years War series of English-French wars (1337–1453), in which England lost all of its possessions in France except Calais (lost to France in 1558).

marsala a dry or sweet, amber-colored fortified wine made in western Sicily.

Piacenza commune in north Italy, in Emilia-Romagna, on the Po River.

Tosca title of Puccini opera.

Modena commune in Emilia-Romagna region of north Italy.

Frisco (slang) San Francisco.

Torino Italian name for Turin, commune in the Piedmont region of northwest Italy, on the Po River.

Normal school a school, usually with a two-year program, for train-ing high school graduates to be elementary schoolteachers.

Chapter XX

Summary

Lieutenant Henry and Catherine Barkley attend the horse races with Helen Ferguson and Crowell Rodgers, the American soldier wounded when he tried to retrieve a souvenir, as well as Mr. and Mrs. Meyers.

Commentary

Hemingway here reiterates Catherine Barkley's heroic status; she is distressed by the rigged racetrack betting in which Meyers is involved. "I don't like this crooked racing!" Catherine declares. She suggests to Lieutenant Henry that they bet on a horse they've never heard of, and although it finishes fifth, she feels "so much cleaner." Note that, as the horses pass in the race during which Henry and Catherine have distanced themselves from the crooked betting, they see the mountains in the distance—a very subtle reminder of the author's geographical dichotomy between pure mountains and corrupt plains. Again, while Henry is tolerant of a certain amount of corruption, Catherine demands purity.

This chapter also foreshadows the separate peace that Henry and Catherine will declare later in the novel. After separating from the others and betting on the horse unlikely to win, she asks him if he likes it better when they're alone, explaining "I felt very lonely when they were all there."

Glossary

San Siro a famous Milan racetrack.

paddock an enclosure at a racetrack, where horses are saddled.

elastic barrier modern starting-gate.

pari-mutuel a system of betting on races in which those backing the winners divide, in proportion to their wagers, the total amount bet, minus a percentage for the track operators, taxes, etc.

Chapter XXI

Summary

Lieutenant Henry is ordered to return to the front after three weeks' convalescent leave. Before he leaves, Catherine Barkley tells him she is three months pregnant.

Commentary

Chapter XXI, which takes place at summer's end, is enormously important dramatically, as it introduces two central turning points in rapid succession: Lieutenant Henry being ordered back to the front and Catherine Barkley's revelation that she is three months pregnant.

Structurally, this chapter is one of the most important in the novel. The official letter sent to Lieutenant Henry tells him and us that the story's idyllic central section will soon reach its conclusion. This is especially bad news considering the information related at the start of Chapter XXI: that the Allies are faring poorly not only locally, but also on the Western and Russian Fronts, against the Germans. Worse, the British major with whom Henry chats predicts that the Germans will invade Italy. The scenario that Henry is about to re-enter will be the photo-negative of his joyous summertime love affair with Catherine Barkley.

Obviously Catherine's pregnancy constitutes an enormously significant plot development as well. Now there are consequences to the affair, and responsibilities associated with it. Catherine reasserts her belief, introduced in the prior chapter, that "there's only us two and in the world there's all the rest of them," but this is patently untrue, inasmuch as another life has entered the picture.

Character Insight

In terms of characterization, the notion of Catherine's special bravery is introduced explicitly here. With characteristic modesty, she suggests she would like to be brave, and Henry shows surprising self-awareness by comparing his own bravery to the talents of a mediocre baseball player. (Recall his cocky statement near the start of *A Farewell to Arms* to the effect that the war could not affect him.) Yet Henry still has living and learning to do: When he naively suggests that "Nothing ever happens to the brave," the more-experienced Catherine counters with the statement, "They die, of course"—ominous foreshadowing, and yet another reason to read on. The novel is like an efficient machine that Hemingway refuels constantly so that it (and therefore our interest in it) remains ever-kinetic.

Glossary

Hun term of contempt applied to German soldiers, especially in WWI.

the Trentino region of north Italy.

Corriere Della Sera (Italian) Evening Courier, a newspaper.

dressing-gown a loose robe for wear when one is not fully clothed, as before dressing or when lounging.

The American news was all training camps It is unclear whether this refers to spring training prior to the baseball season, to the training of newly enlisted soldiers, or to both.

"I did everything. I took everything but it didn't make any difference." Catherine has tried to prevent pregnancy with various forms of contraception that would now be considered unscientific and ineffective.

Chapter XXII

Summary

Lieutenant Henry is diagnosed with what is probably hepatitis. Discovering empty liquor bottles in his armoire, Nurse Van Campen accuses him of drinking to excess so as to contract the disease and thereby remain in the hospital, which Henry denies. As a result of his illness, he must cancel his planned vacation with Catherine.

Commentary

It is raining hard on the day after Catherine Barkley's announcement of her pregnancy, the symbolism of which seems undeniable. Nurse Van Campen's theory that a man would contract a painful illness in order to avoid fighting underlines just how far some indeed will go in order to avoid combat. Again, Lieutenant Henry is not alone in his ambivalence about the war.

Glossary

the jaundice colloquial reference to a disease, usually hepatitis, causing the eyeballs, the skin, and the urine to become abnormally yellowish as a result of increased amounts of bile pigments in the blood.

Pallanza town on Lake Maggiore.

Lago Maggiore Lake Maggiore, which spans the border between Italy and Switzerland, northwest of Milan.

Stresa town on Lake Maggiore.

kümmel a colorless liqueur flavored with caraway seeds, anise, cumin, etc.

Chapter XXIII

Summary

On their last evening together in Milan, Lieutenant Henry and Catherine Barkley take a room in a hotel after he buys a pistol.

Commentary

We have been introduced earlier to the theme that Catherine Barkley has no conventional religion, and it is reiterated here in her refusal of Lieutenant Henry's invitation to enter the Milan Cathedral. The author contrasts Henry and Catherine to the soldier and his girlfriend standing together in the shelter of the church; the former have no conventional faith to protect them. Remember that the officers at the front took their refuge in houses of prostitution—obviously not an option for Henry and Catherine. What they have is their love for one another.

Literary Device

Henry buys a pistol to replace the one lost when he was injured. As this is the second time that our attention has been directed to Henry's pistol, we can only assume that it is an object of some importance. Notice that Henry refuses the offer of a "used, very cheap" sword. "I'm going to the front," he explains, and the proprietor of the armorer's shop replies, "Oh yes, then you won't need a sword." As Hemingway has made clear from the novel's first scene, this is not a storybook war in which combatants carry swords, much less use them: World War I is modern, unromantic, brutal. During Henry and Catherine's trip from the armorer's to the hotel near the train station, the fog that has covered the city from the start of the chapter turns to rain, the novel's symbol of death.

Staying in a hotel room for less than an entire night, with a man who is not her husband, makes Catherine feel like a whore. (The room's bordello-like décor surely doesn't help matters.) Here we are reminded of Henry's leave from the front early in the novel, which he spent for the most part in exciting but unfulfilling encounters with prostitutes, and we realize how much he has matured since.

With regard to the Hemingway style, notice that only now, after months of intimacy, does Henry learn that Catherine has a father; she learns, in turn, that he doesn't. Again, Hemingway's novels and stories are remarkable, and distinctively modern, for their lack of exposition. Though *A Farewell to Arms* contains almost no information about Henry's life prior to the war, much less Catherine's, we don't particularly miss it, as the present action is so compelling.

Glossary

musette a small bag of canvas or leather for toilet articles, etc., worn suspended from a shoulder strap.

Mürren alpine resort.

woodcock a migratory European shorebird, with short legs and a long bill: it is hunted as game.

St. Estephe a type of wine.

purée de marron chestnuts ground or mashed until smooth.

zabaione a frothy dessert or sauce made of eggs, sugar, and wine, typically Marsala, beaten together over boiling water.

Hotel Cavour a fancy Milanese hotel.

gout a hereditary form of recurrent, acute arthritis with swelling and severe pain, resulting from a disturbance of uric acid metabolism and characterized by an excess of uric acid in the blood and deposits of uric acid salts usually in the joints of the feet and hands, especially in the big toe.

"But at my back I always hear/Time's winged chariot hurrying near" Lieutenant Henry quotes from "To His Coy Mistress," a lyric poem by Andrew Marvell (see below). The reference to the poem itself, about a woman who is sexually unavailable, is ironic, considering all of Henry and Catherine's premarital sexual activity. But the lines themselves are consistent with the sense of doom that pervades the novel.

Marvell Andrew Marvell (1621–78), English poet.

Chapter XXIV

Summary

Lieutenant Henry and Catherine Barkley say goodbye at the Milan train station. Henry has paid a soldier to save him a seat on the train, but to avoid trouble, he gives his seat to a captain. The train departs for the front.

Commentary

The last chapter in Book Two is short and remarkably unsentimental, considering that it marks the end of Lieutenant Henry and Catherine Barkley's idyll—and, for all we know, the end of their affair, as Henry is returning to the front. Hemingway resists the urge to milk melodrama from the lovers' goodbye, and this is consistent with the characters themselves and their stoic behavior up to this point. Notice that it continues to rain as they bid one another farewell. In fact, Catherine's last act in this part of the novel is to signal to Henry that he should step in out of the rain.

Glossary

Brescia commune in Lombardy, north Italy, at the foot of the Alps.

Book Three
Chapter XXV

Summary

Lieutenant Henry returns to the front, where he is told by the major that the summer has been bad for the Italian forces. Henry is reunited with Rinaldi, and the two friends go to dinner at the mess, where the latter baits the priest aggressively.

Commentary

In many ways, this chapter recapitulates the opening of the novel: Again, it is autumn, and "the trees were all bare and the roads were muddy." Rinaldi still torments the priest. Two things have changed, however: the fortunes of the Italian troops and Lieutenant Henry himself. Of the latter, Rinaldi observes, "You act like a married man."

Literary Device

Hemingway here employs the character of Rinaldi as a kind of foil, or contrast, to Henry. Henry departed the front due to his injury and has matured as a result of the love he shares with Catherine Barkley. Rinaldi, left behind, has grown increasingly bitter and hostile due to the stress of the war. "This war is killing me," he says, and the statement may be more than metaphorical. Rinaldi believes he has contracted syphilis (a terminal illness), presumably from sex with prostitutes. Again, the author links sex and death, via war.

Glossary

Caporetto village in present-day Slovenia, the scene of a battle in World War I in which the Italian army was defeated by Austro-German forces (1917).

the French will hog them all The major predicts, correctly, that most of the American troops will be sent to the Western Front.

harlot prostitute.

"Does she—?" The dash here takes the place of a vulgar term for a sexual act. Throughout the novel, Hemingway will substitute dashes for obscene expressions. (Ironically, *A Farewell to Arms* was nevertheless banned in Boston because of its supposed obscenity.)

the snake of reason a reference to the serpent in the story of the Garden of Eden, from the Book of Genesis in the Bible.

The apple the fruit of knowledge, offered by the serpent to Eve. When she shared the apple with Adam, they were cast out of Eden by God.

" . . . two other things; one is bad for my work and the other is over in half an hour or fifteen minutes." drinking and sex, presumably.

Saint Paul the Apostle Paul.

Purissimo very pure.

Sporchissimo very dirty.

" . . . Saint Paul . . . was a rounder and a chaser and then when he was no longer hot he said it was no good. When he was finished he made the rules for those of us who are still hot." According the Book of Acts in the New Testament, St. Paul was originally a persecutor of Christians named Saul; he saw Jesus Christ on the road to Damascus and was converted.

"What are you eating meat for? . . . Don't you know it's Friday?" Traditionally, Roman Catholics refrain from eating meat on Friday.

"What if I have it. Everybody has it. The whole world's got it. First . . . it's a little pimple. Then we notice a rash between the shoulders. Then we notice nothing at all. We put our faith in mercury." A description of the symptoms and treatment of syphilis.

bread pudding with hard sauce a custard dessert made with pieces of bread, raisins, or other fruit, etc., served in this case with a sweet, creamy mixture of butter, powdered sugar, and a flavoring such as vanilla extract, rum, or brandy.

Chapter XXVI

Summary

In Lieutenant Henry's room after dinner, he and the priest discuss the war.

Commentary

Character Insight

This chapter, written mainly in untagged dialogue, serves primarily as an index of Lieutenant Henry's growth. Near the end of their talk, Henry agrees with the priest when the latter says "I don't believe in victory any more." Henry still asserts that he doesn't believe in defeat, either. And yet he suggests, philosophically, that defeat "may be better." The Henry at the novel's opening was incapable of such a statement. The priest too has changed, "surer of himself" now than when Henry left the front.

Chapter XXVII

Summary

Lieutenant Henry reconnoiters the area. That night the Austrians (and, as later becomes evident, the Germans) begin an offensive, bombarding the Italian forces and eventually breaking through the Italian lines near Caporetto. The Italians begin to retreat, and the ambulance drivers prepare to travel to Pordenone, beyond the Tagliamento River.

Commentary

The entry of the Germans is a turning point in the narrative. Lieutenant Henry tells us, "The word Germans was something to be frightened of. We did not want to have anything to do with the Germans."

Literary
Device

The mountains-plains dichotomy is further developed, as Henry tells the driver named Gino that he does not believe a war can be fought and won in the mountains. Thus the mountains emerge here not only as a place of purity versus the corruption of the plains, but as a place of refuge, as well. This will be important later in the story.

"What has been done this summer cannot have been done in vain," Gino tells Henry. He refers to the fighting, but the statement has a double meaning for the reader, applying to the love shared by Henry and Catherine Barkley, as well.

Theme

One long paragraph in this chapter summarizes Henry's character and a theme of the novel: "I was always embarrassed by the words sacred, glorious, and sacrifice and the expression in vain," Henry tells us. "Abstract words such as glory, honor, courage or hallow were obscene beside the concrete names of villages, the numbers of roads, the names of rivers, the numbers of regiments and the dates." The words Henry mentions, which he might have used himself at the story's beginning, now ring hollow as a result of his actual wartime experience.

Hemingway has struggled in *A Farewell to Arms* to write a new kind of war story, and here he makes that effort explicit. This paragraph explicitly states the writer's stylistic credo, as well. Throughout his writing career, Hemingway always favored the concrete over the abstract, the specific over the vague. And his radical preference for the concrete and the specific remains, perhaps, his greatest stylistic legacy—far more influential than his use of a limited vocabulary or simple and/or compound, rather than complex, sentences.

Literary Device

Notice that it rains almost continuously during this chapter, during which the tide turns and the Italians begin to retreat in the face of the Austrian-German onslaught. The rain turns to snow one evening, holding out hope that the offensive will cease, but it quickly melts and the rain resumes. During a discussion among the drivers about the wine they are drinking with dinner, the driver named Aymo says, "To-morrow maybe we drink rainwater." Hemingway has by this time developed the rain symbolism to such a degree that the reader experiences a genuine sense of foreboding.

Glossary

dolce (Italian) dessert.

Lom town near the border between present-day Bulgaria and Romania.

Ternova ridge in present-day Slovenia.

Babbitting metal a soft white metal of tin, lead, copper, and antimony in various proportions, used to reduce frictions as in bearings.

Croat a person born or living in Croatia, a country in southeast Europe that was at one time part of Austria-Hungary.

Magyar a member of the people constituting the main ethnic group in Hungary.

"Alto piano . . . but no piano" (Italian) "Upland plain . . . but no plain."

Brindisi a seaport in Apulia, southeast Italy, on the Adriatic.

dogfish any of various small sharks. Lieutenant Henry means to be insulting.

Pordenone a town in northeast Italy, between the Piave and Tagliamento Rivers.

monkey suit (slang) a uniform.

"We may drink—" As before, the dash replaces an obscenity, in this case a slang reference to urine, most likely.

"Tomorrow maybe we'll sleep in—" The dash replaces an obscenity.

Tagliamento a river in the Venetia region of northeast Italy, to the west of Udine, that flows south to the Adriatic Sea.

Chapter XXVIII

Summary

The ambulance drivers retreat from the enemy attack in a long, slow-moving column of vehicles. They pick up two Italian engineer-sergeants and two teenage girls. Falling asleep in the car, Lieutenant Henry dreams of Catherine Barkley. Finally, the ambulances pull off the main road and stop at an abandoned farmhouse, where Henry and the others scavenge breakfast.

Commentary

In Hemingway's description of the retreat from Caporetto, he focuses on the concrete and specific: a sewing machine in the back of a cart, for instance.

In terms of the narrative, the two Italian sergeants picked up by one of the ambulances will prove central in the story to come. Innocuous-seeming at first, they begin to appear sinister at chapter's end, when it appears they haven't shared their breakfast with the others at the abandoned farmhouse. Lieutenant Henry's alienation from the cause is emphasized by the sergeants' disbelief that he is not Italian-American. Instead he is described as "North American English," which reminds the reader of his bond with the British Catherine Barkley. Indeed, Lieutenant Henry thinks and then dreams of her, a reminder of the novel's love angle as well as a recapitulation of the Joycean stream-of-consciousness style that Hemingway employs periodically.

"A retreat was no place for two virgins," Henry tells the reader, subtly reminding us of Hemingway's love-sex-war-death continuum. Someone with no sexual experience is especially vulnerable in wartime, the writer seems to be telling us. Of course, everyone is vulnerable, as Henry reminds the reader mid-way through the chapter; if the weather clears, a slow-moving column of vehicles will be pitifully unprotected from the bombs of enemy planes. From the safety and security of the American hospital in Milan, we have been transported in a few short chapters to a life-and-death situation.

Glossary

Sorella (Italian) sister.

"Blow, blow, ye western wind . . . Christ, that my love were in my arms and I in my bed again. That my love Catherine. That my sweet love Catherine down might rain. Blow her again to me." Falling asleep in the cab of the ambulance, Lieutenant Henry recites to himself a garbled version of a poem from the sixteenth century, the author of which is unknown. The best-known lines from this poem are as follows: "O Western wind, when wilt thou blow,/That the small rain down can rain?/Christ, that my love were in my arms/And I in my bed again!" Note the portentous rain imagery.

Chapter XXIX

Summary

When one of the ambulances becomes stuck in the mud, the two sergeants refuse to assist in the effort to dislodge it and instead try to strike out on their own. Henry orders them to halt, and when they continue walking, Henry fires, wounding one; the ambulance driver Bonello uses Henry's pistol to finish the job. The group abandons all three ambulances and sets out on foot.

Commentary

Literary
Device

Chapter XXIX features one of the story's most dramatic and significant turning points, in Lieutenant Henry's shooting the deserting Italian sergeant. This is the first time, in this war novel, that the protagonist has fired a shot (using the pistol bought with Catherine Barkley on their last night together). And yet he fires the gun at a member of his own side rather than at an enemy. The irony will intensify in the next chapter, as Henry himself stands on the verge of being shot for desertion. The discipline of the front is replaced by a ragged retreat, and now the situation verges on complete disorder.

Again Hemingway emphasizes the difference between this war and those of myth and legend. The ambulance driver Piani suggests that the cavalry will appear, to which Henry replies "I don't think they've got any cavalry." Note in particular that the mud introduced in the first chapter of the novel has returned as a kind of antagonist here: It is responsible for the disabling of the ambulances, which in turn leads to the death of the deserting officer.

And yet the story is no less exciting for its lack of old-time heroics. Hemingway increases the tension in this chapter by telling us that enemy planes have passed overhead en route to bombing the road where the column of retreat is moving, and later in the chapter, Henry thinks he hears firing in the distance.

Glossary

Imola town in the Emilia-Romagna region of north Italy.

Chapter XXX

Summary

Hiking toward Udine, the ambulance drivers Lieutenant Henry, Aymo, Bonello, and Piani spot German soldiers. Aymo is shot to death, presumably by Italians firing in error. Bonello flees, to surrender to the Germans. Finally having crossed the Tagliamento River, Henry observes that Italian officers are being shot by the military police for deserting their troops. He also fears being taken for a German spy. He dives into the river, deserting the Italian army.

Commentary

This chapter serves as the climax of the novel, a point of no return after which all the action is, in a sense, downhill. First we saw Italian soldiers shot by their superior (Lieutenant Henry) because they were deserting. Here, Aymo is shot by his compatriots by accident, out of fear and incompetence. At chapter's end, Italian soldiers are shooting other Italian soldiers at random, simply because the latter are officers. Chaos is on the loose.

Therefore, and because Hemingway has been preparing us for this moment from the scene early in the novel when the English nurse was puzzled by his very membership in the Italian army, we do not question Lieutenant Henry's decision to desert. As he tells Bonello, "We are in more danger from Italians than from Germans." Indeed, at the end of Chapter XXX, it is all but certain that if he does not flee, Henry will be executed by the Italian military police. He really has no choice.

Also, Henry's loyalty has never been to the Italian army at large anyway, but rather to those individuals with whom he has lived and worked. The ambulance group having disbanded, he feels he has no obligation to continue on behalf of the cause—which is, after all, an abstraction.

Note the theme of declaring a separate peace. As verbalized by the Italian soldiers, who think they can end the war by throwing away their rifles, it sounds naïve and foolish. It will prove to be so by the end of the novel. Notice also the reliance of the military police on words like "sacred soil" and "fruits of victory"—precisely the abstractions that Henry told us, a few chapters back, that he mistrusts. "Have you ever been in a retreat?" asks the lieutenant colonel who is about to be shot. A retreat is concrete and specific—it is something real. The lofty terms used by the M.P.s are proof that they haven't had the sort of experience that Henry has gained over the course of the novel.

Glossary

Campoformio Campoformido, town in northeast Italy, south of Udine.

Cividale Cividale del Friuli, town in northeast Italy between Udine and the Isonzo River.

"A basso gli ufficiali!" (Italian) "Down with the officers!"

Brigata di Pace (Italian) Peace Brigade.

"Viva la Pace!" (Italian) "Long live peace!"

caisson a two-wheeled wagon for transporting ammunition.

carbines rifles with a short barrel, originally for use by cavalry.

Chapter XXXI

Summary

Despite a powerful current, Frederic—no longer Lieutenant—Henry manages to swim ashore. He crosses part of the Venetian plain on foot. He boards a moving train, hiding among guns stored beneath a tarpaulin.

Commentary

This chapter is mainly connective. Notice, however, that Frederic Henry's desertion is illustrated with concrete specifics: gunless now, he pulls the insigniae from the sleeves of his uniform.

Style & Language

Hemingway's masterful way with action manifests itself at the start of Chapter XXXI and when Henry boards the train. Also note the author's curious use of *you* and *we* in what is otherwise a first-person-singular ("I") narration. While swimming, Henry describes himself as *you,* and then *we.* The effect is of close identification with the reader—of our implication in his actions, even. We are all Frederic Henry, Hemingway seems to be implying.

Glossary

Latisana town on the Tagliamento River in northeast Italy.

San Vito San Vito al Tagliamento, a town to the west of the River Tagliamento in northeast Italy.

Portogruaro a town in northeast Italy, just south of San Vito al Tagliamento.

grummet a ring of rope or metal used to fasten the edge of a sail to its stay, hold an oar in place, etc.

Chapter XXXII

Summary

Frederic Henry lies hidden amid the guns beneath the canvas covering the train car and thinks about deserting and about Catherine Barkley.

Commentary

Book Three ends quietly, with Frederic Henry's thoughts rendered in a Joycean stream-of-consciousness style. (Note the use, again, of the second-person point-of-view in the narration.) Henry justifies his desertion to himself, the desertion that in a sense he has been rationalizing from the start of the novel. "You were out of it now," he thinks. "You had no more obligation." This, of course, is the episode that gives the novel its title—a bit ironically, considering that it takes place on a train car transporting guns.

It is typical of Hemingway's heroes not to bear grudges, and Henry is no exception: "Anger was washed away in the river along with any obligation," he tells us. As the story continues, he will bear the Italians no ill will—or, if he feels any resentment, he will at least refrain from expressing it.

Book Four
Chapter XXXIII

Summary

Frederic Henry arrives, incognito, in Milan. Catherine Barkley and Nurse Ferguson are absent from the hospital, having gone on holiday to Stresa. Henry seeks help from his friend Simmons, the music student.

Commentary

Hemingway maintains the dramatic tension in this short, introductory chapter, as Frederic Henry discovers that everyone he meets is aware of the retreat. Many seem as well to be attuned to the issue of desertion, and significantly, it doesn't matter much to them. The bartender, for instance, advises Henry not to wear his coat, as the place where he removed his insignia is clearly visible.

Two themes that run through much of Hemingway's work are dramatized in Chapter XXXIII: the decency of the common man and the value of friendship. Although a stranger, the bartender offers to help Henry, as does his friend Simmons. The porter at the hospital not only offers to assist Henry but refuses money for doing so. Despite Henry's alienation and Anglophilia, scenes like this one protect Hemingway from the potential charge that he is anti-Italian in *A Farewell to Arms*; it is the Italian army, specifically the military police, of which he is critical.

The writer continues to evoke entire scenes from a few concrete details. Henry tells us, of the wine shop where he first stops for coffee, that "It smelled of early morning, of swept dust, spoons in coffee glasses and the wet circles left by wine-glasses." Like the brick dust on the cheese during the Austrian bombardment in Chapter IX, these specifics bring the scene alive for us.

Glossary

Porta Magenta one of the gates of the city of Milan.

the Lyrico Milanese theater.

Helvetia Switzerland.

"Africana" song title.

Chapter XXXIV

Summary

Frederic Henry travels via train to the resort town of Stresa, where he finds Catherine Barkley in a hotel dining room with Nurse Ferguson. Henry and Catherine spend the night together in his hotel room.

Commentary

Finally Frederic Henry and Catherine Barkley are reunited, but the atmosphere is very different from that of their last meeting in Milan. Although Catherine is somewhat oblivious to it, danger hovers everywhere. Henry characterizes himself as a masquerader in civilian clothes, a truant from school, and finally a criminal. "It's not deserting from the army. It's only the Italian army," Catherine reassures him, and us, continuing the pattern of rationalization begun near the start of the novel.

Notice the change—the growth—in Henry's character, demonstrated at the start of Chapter XXXIV. Of the hostile aviators with whom he shares a train compartment, he says that "in the old days I would have insulted them and picked a fight." Now, no longer insecure due to his experiences in love and war, he does not even feel insulted.

It is raining while Henry rides the train to Stresa, raining when he arrives, and raining while Henry and Catherine spend the night together in his hotel room. Remember Catherine's vision of herself dead in the rain. And note the undeniably ominous quality of what is perhaps the novel's best-known, most-quoted passage, which follows soon afterward:

> "If people bring so much courage to this world the world has to kill them to break them, so of course it kills them. The world breaks every one and afterward many are strong at the broken places. But those that will not break it kills. It kills the very good and the very gentle and the very brave impartially. If you are none of these you can be sure it will kill you too but there will be no special hurry."

Style & Language

Here the author writes in a different mode, one of lofty abstractions that contrast strongly with the concrete details he usually favors. Note, however, that even at his most philosophical, Hemingway still favors simple, colloquial language.

"I had made a separate peace," Henry tells himself in Chapter XXXIV. The question that the last third of *A Farewell to Arms* addresses is this: Can one make a separate peace?

Glossary

Gallarate town in Lombardy region of north Italy, between Milan and Lake Maggiore.

letto matrimoniale (Italian) literally, "marriage bed"; a double bed.

borghese (Italian) civilian clothes.

mufti ordinary clothes, especially worn by one who normally wears, or has long worn, a military or other uniform.

Chapter XXXV

Summary

Frederic Henry fishes on the lake with the barman at his hotel while Catherine Barkley visits Nurse Ferguson. After spending the afternoon in bed with Catherine, Henry plays billiards with his friend, the 94-year-old Count Greffi.

Commentary

This is a transitional chapter in the narrative. Although apparently fishing with the barman, Frederic Henry is also reconnoitering an escape route from Italy into neutral Switzerland. The intensity of his love for Catherine Barkley is emphasized as well; he tells her that he has nothing when they're apart and that he feels faint from loving her so much. When he loses her at novel's end, the reader's own feelings of loss on Henry's behalf will therefore be intense.

Character Insight

In fact, as his talk with Count Greffi reveals, the once-indifferent Henry has truly found something to believe in. He tells the Count that what he values most is someone he loves and that he "might become very devout," elaborating that his religious feeling comes at night. Like Catherine, Henry has made a religion of their love.

The justification by Hemingway of Henry's desertion from the army continues in the form of the wise Count's opinion that the war is stupid. Henry continues to feel strange in civilian clothes, and he is disinclined to discuss the war at all, betraying lingering feelings of guilt. Yet the author discourages us from truly questioning, and therefore becoming distracted by, the morality of Henry's abandonment of the cause.

Glossary

San Dona town on the Piave River, in Italy just east of Venice.

Cortina D'Ampezzo town in the Carnac Alps, in Italy due north of Venice.

Cadore region in the Carnac Alps, east of Cortina D'Ampezzo.

Metternich Prince von (1773–1859), Austrian statesman and diplomat.

Isola Bella an island in Lake Maggiore, on the Italian side of the border.

strike the pull on the line by a fish seizing or snatching at bait.

gunwale the upper edge of the side of a ship or boat.

Abyssinia former name for Ethiopia.

L'heure du cocktail (French) cocktail hour.

Othello with his occupation gone The hero of Shakespeare's tragedy Othello commands the Venetian forces who travel to Cypress to fight the Turks. Othello's wife, Desdemona, dies near the conclusion of the play.

franc the basic monetary unit of Belgim, France, Liechtenstein, Luxembourg, and Switzerland.

"Le Feu" by a Frenchman, Barbusse . . . "Mr. Britling Sees Through It" contemporary novels.

Croyant (French) believing.

Chapter XXXVI

Summary

The barman appears at Frederic Henry's hotel room late at night to tell him that he will be arrested as a deserter in the morning. Henry and Catherine Barkley quickly prepare for their escape into Switzerland.

Commentary

Notice again the decency of the common man; not only does the barman inform Frederic Henry of his impending arrest, he also all but gives him his fishing boat, presumably endangering his own safety in the process.

Literary Device

Now the rain symbolism and Catherine Barkley (or at least her expected baby) seem on a direct collision course. Notice the following juxtaposition: "She was beginning to be a little big with the child and she did not want me to see her. I dressed hearing the rain on the windows." The author does hold out hope, however, telling us that although the wind across the lake is cold and wet, "it was snowing in the mountains." Remember that snow is the novel's symbol of tranquility and that the mountains stand not just for purity but for safety, as well.

Glossary

quay a wharf, usually of concrete or stone, used for loading and unloading ships.

Luino, Cannero, Cannobio, Tranzano ... Brissago ... Monte Tamara towns and villages along the shore of Lake Maggiore.

Isola Madre an island in Lake Maggiore.

Pallanza a town on the shore of Lake Maggiore.

Mattarone Italian name for the Matterhorn, a mountain in the Pennine Alps, on the Swiss-Italian border.

Chapter XXXVII

Summary

Through the stormy night, Frederic Henry and Catherine Barkley row across the lake from Italy into Switzerland. The following day they are arrested and briefly detained, after which they are released.

Commentary

This chapter, the climax of Book Four, deftly combines thrilling action and nail-biting suspense with comic relief—not to mention relief in general, when Frederic Henry and Catherine Barkley are released by the police, their escape from Italy an apparent success. Notice how Hemingway combines the nighttime setting, stormy conditions (include the symbolically significant rain), the physical challenge of rowing for miles and miles, Catherine's vulnerable condition ("Watch the oar doesn't pop you in the tummy"), and the threat of arrest by patrolling customs officers to yield drama of the highest order. The boat journey itself shows the influence of a short story by one of Hemingway's favorite writers, Stephen Crane's "The Open Boat."

Literary Device

The comic relief provided by Henry and Catherine's masquerade as students of art and architecture, followed by the winter-sports argument between the Swiss police, can justly be compared to similar scenes in Shakespeare—the gravedigger scene in *Hamlet*, for instance. Such material provides the reader or audience with a respite from the emotional intensity of the unfolding drama. Moreover, when tragedy finally strikes, it will be that much more powerful because of its contrast to the comic material that went before.

Character Insight

With regard to characterization, Catherine's extraordinary fortitude is very much in evidence here. Despite her fairly advanced pregnancy, she not only travels through the November night in an open boat but also offers to hold the umbrella so it will serve as a sail. She steers and bails and even rows for a while, always maintaining a sense of humor. Is she one of "the very brave" that Henry has recently told us the world must kill?

Glossary

Intra a town on the shore of Lake Maggiore.

Castagnola a town on the shore of Lake Maggiore.

guardia di finanza (Italian) customs service.

catch crabs in rowing, to fail to clear the water on the recovery stroke accidentally, thereby unbalancing the boat or impeding its movement.

Locarno a town in south Switzerland, on Lake Maggiore. Significantly, it would be the site of a peace conference in 1925.

Wengen a winter resort.

Montreaux a town in west Switzerland, on Lake Geneva.

luge a small racing sled on which one or two riders lie face up with the feet forward.

piste (Italian) tracks or trails.

Engadine the valley of the upper Inn River, east Switzerland; site of many resorts.

stazione (Italian) station.

There's no hole in my side a reference to Jesus Christ, wounded in the side by a Roman spear. Henry's sacrilegious joke is inspired by his blistered palms, which recall Christ's stigmata.

Chapter XXXVIII

Summary

Frederic Henry and Catherine Barkley move into a chalet on a mountain above Montreaux. Henry reads newspaper reports that the fighting goes badly for the Italian side.

Commentary

Regarding the novel's symbolism, notice that snow comes unusually late during the winter described. As a result, the fighting continues. Frederic Henry says that the war "seemed as far away as the football games of someone else's college," and yet he worries about his compatriots Rinaldi and the priest. "I don't want to think about the war," he tells Catherine. "I'm through with it." Still, Henry has difficulty sleeping at night, presumably a result of guilt over his desertion.

Literary Device

Eventually, however, two benign strands of symbolism intertwine as Henry and Catherine find themselves in the mountains, with snow all around. Thus they have achieved, momentarily at least, a life of both purity and safety. (The landscape strongly recalls that of the priest's Abruzzi hometown as described near the start of the novel.) And indeed, due to Hemingway's remarkable powers of description, Chapter XXXVIII and those immediately afterwards positively radiate contentment. This is a clever storytelling strategy on the writer's part, as what follows will be that much more horrific by contrast with this idyllic section.

Henry again suggests marriage, and Catherine again resists, as she doesn't want to be a bride while so obviously pregnant. Not that it would matter much, as Henry and Catherine know almost no one in Montreaux. And yet their isolation brings them closer together than ever. In fact, Catherine suggests they wear their hair the same length, so as to be more alike. "Oh darling," she says, "I want you so much I want to be you too." Henry replies, "You are. We're the same one."

Literary Device

This chapter also contains foreshadowing of an explicit, technical, and distinctly ominous nature: Catherine's doctor tells her she has narrow hips, which could be problematic with regard to childbirth.

Glossary

Chalet a type of Swiss house, built of wood with balconies and overhanging eaves.

Rhone a river flowing from southwest Switzerland south through France into the Gulf of Lions.

Dent du Midi mountain in the Alps.

"Hoyle" a book of rules and instructions for indoor games, especially card games, originally compiled by Edmond Hoyle (1672–1769), English authority on card games and chess.

Zurich capital of canton in north Switzerland, on the Lake of Zurich.

Chernex, Fontanivent alpine villages.

grebe a diving or swimming bird with broadly lobed toes and legs set far back on the body.

Munich a city in southeast Germany, capital of the state of Bavaria.

Niagara Falls a large waterfall on the Niagara River, between New York State and Canada; a traditional honeymoon destination.

The Woolworth Building a New York skyscraper designed by Cass Gilbert and built in 1913; until 1931 it was the tallest building in the world. The Woolworth Building was known as the "cathedral of commerce," which makes Catherine's desire to go there vaguely ironic after her refusal to enter the actual cathedral in Milan.

M.O.B. Montreaux Oberland Bernois railway.

Chapter XXXIX

Summary

Frederic Henry and Catherine Barkley talk about family.

Commentary

The idyll continues—as do the relentless hints of doom to come. "What do you want to do? Ruin me?" Frederic Henry wants to know. Catherine Barkley's reply: "Yes. I want to ruin you."

Glossary

glühwein (German) mulled wine.

chamois a small goat antelope of the mountains of Europe and the Caucasus, having straight horns with the tips bent backward.

Dent du Jaman mountain in the Alps.

Chapter XL

Summary

At winter's end, Frederic Henry and Catherine Barkley leave the mountains for a hotel in Lausanne.

Commentary

Literary Device

Symbolism alerts us that Frederic Henry and Catherine Barkley's second idyll now nears its conclusion. Winter, nature's cease-fire, is at an end. "In the night it started raining," Henry tells us, reporting that it does so even high up on the mountain. Of the train trip to Lausanne, he reports that "Looking out the window toward where we had lived you could not see the mountains for the clouds." Thus there is no longer any refuge for the couple from death. The question at this point is, is it the death of their love affair? Or that of their unborn child? It is not clear yet, but the sense of foreboding in Chapter XL is so extreme as to be almost unbearable.

Glossary

Lausanne a city in west Switzerland, on Lake Geneva.

Vevey a town in west Switzerland, on Lake Geneva. Significantly, it is the setting at the start of Henry James's Daisy Miller, a story that ends with the tragic death of its heroine.

cogwheel railway a railway for a very steep grade with traction supplied by a central cogged rail that meshes with a cogwheel on the engine.

Ouchy town near Lausanne, in west Switzerland.

Chapter XLI

Summary

In the novel's final chapter, Frederic Henry takes Catherine Barkley to the hospital, where she experiences a protracted and agonizing childbirth. First the baby dies, having choked on its umbilical cord. Then, as a result of multiple hemorrhages, Catherine dies as well.

Commentary

Chapter XLI achieves its tragic and powerful effect mainly by following through on the painstaking preparation of all the chapters that have gone before. For instance, the nurse's instructions that Catherine change into a nightgown upon her arrival at the hospital remind us of the nightgown bought for the hotel stay on the couple's last night in Milan, perhaps even hinting that it was on that evening that Catherine conceived the baby she is about to bear. Similarly, card games among the patrons of the café where Henry eats during the baby's ill-fated delivery remind us of his gross misunderstanding at the affair's beginning that it was a game, like chess or bridge.

Notice that Catherine tells the admitting nurse she has no religion. About her caesarian operation, Henry tells us that "It looked like a drawing of the Inquisition." Admitting once again that he himself is an agnostic, Henry briefly regrets that the baby was not baptized, then changes his mind. There is no point in believing in God in a world that senselessly kills Aymo, Rinaldi, the baby—and "Now Catherine would die." It is a world like the burning campfire log that Henry describes, swarming with ants that he cannot save despite the impulse "to be a messiah."

Still, as anyone would, he tries bargaining with God in his desperation at Catherine's impending death. She, on the other hand, retains the courage of her convictions to the end. "Just you," she requests of Henry in response to his offer of a priest's visit. Despite everything, love is her religion until the instant she dies.

The word "brave" and the concept of Catherine's bravery appear throughout the chapter, to horrifying effect, as Henry has already shared with us his viewpoint that the very brave are destined to die. "I'm all going to pieces," Catherine tells Henry, reminding us of the novel's best-known passage (see Chapter XXXIV). Moments later, he tells her to be brave, and she responds "I'm not brave any more, darling, I'm all broken. They've broken me."

first Catherine responds to the discomfort of childbirth cheerfully ("When the pains were bad she called them good ones"), consistent with her characterization throughout the story and especially during the perilous escape from Italy. When she cannot smile and joke later, the implication is that her pain must be excruciating. Similarly, Henry has borne up under so much wartime suffering, yet he is unable to watch the caesarian operation: proof that it is grisly indeed. "This"—suffering and death—"was what people got for loving each other," he tells us, reiterating the author's love-sex-war-death continuum. Note that the war goes on, oblivious, as evinced by the newspaper Henry reads at the café.

With regard to the symbolically-significant weather, when Henry leaves the hospital for lunch, "The day was cloudy but the sun was trying to come through." During the operation, he looks out the window and sees that it is raining. Just after the nurse has told him that the baby is dead, Henry looks outside again and "could see nothing but the dark and the rain falling across the light from the window." Other symbolism in this chapter includes the overturned garbage can containing nothing but "coffee grounds, dust and some dead flowers." A more bleak vision of life can hardly be imagined.

Finally, following the stylistic example of his teacher Gertrude Stein, Hemingway repeats two phrases like a refrain: Catherine's "*Give it to me*," regarding the painkilling nitrous oxide, and Henry's interior "She won't/can't die." The dramatic result: tension is augmented to positively harrowing effect. The writer also makes much stylistic use of James Joyce's stream-of-consciousness technique, as long passages quote directly from Henry's jumbled, panicked thoughts and feelings.

Henry's repeated visits to the local café during Catherine's ordeal not only turn up the tension, as we wonder desperately what is evolving back at the hospital. Also, tragically, they serve for Henry as a kind of unconscious rehearsal for his life after Catherine's death to come. (The writer tested this dynamic in an early story, the justly famous "Hills Like White Elephants.") We know as a result that he will be terribly lonely when she is gone.

In fact, Henry's aloneness begins as soon as Catherine dies: The doctor offers help and companionship, and Henry refuses both. This is consistent with Catherine's own refusal of assistance to the very end. Her answer to Henry's question, "Do you want me to get a priest or any one to come and see you?" is "Just you." Ironically, Henry and Catherine's separate peace has been so successful—in its separateness, at least—that they find themselves without a community to provide support and sustenance in this time of ultimate need. In *A Farewell to Arms,* as well as his other novels and stories, Hemingway chose to emphasize that even when they exist, such communities cannot save us from our own mortality: a bleak vision, indeed.

Glossary

some cylinders . . . a rubber mask attached to a tube   apparatus for delivering nitrous oxide ("laughing gas").

petcock a small faucet or valve.

kirsch a colorless alcoholic drink distilled from the fermented juice of black cherries.

marc the brandy distilled from the refuse of grapes, seeds, other fruits, etc. after pressing; the French counterpart to grappa.

choucroute (French) sauerkraut.

demi demi-blonde beer.

bock a dark beer traditionally drunk in the early spring.

in the mill-race literally, in the channel in which the current of water that drives a mill wheel runs. A colloquialism meaning past the point of no return.

plat du jour (French) special of the day.

CHARACTER ANALYSES

Frederic Henry

In terms of characters and characterization (versus plot and theme), *A Farewell to Arms* is the story of Lieutenant Frederic Henry and the way he grows and changes, lives and learns, in order to catch up to the Nurse Catherine Barkley with respect to experience and the wisdom that it brings. Especially considering that Ernest Hemingway has been accused of misogyny, it is fascinating to note that Catherine is the more mature of the two characters when they meet; therefore, it is Henry who must struggle to match her level of maturity.

Returning from his leave near the start of the novel, Henry knows he should have traveled to the priest's home region of Abruzzi, a "place where the roads were frozen and hard as iron, where it was clear and cold and dry and the snow was dry and powdery and hare-tracks in the snow and the peasants took off their hats and called you Lord and there was good hunting." Instead he has visited bars and whorehouses in the cities of the lowlands. For now, Henry's strategy vis-à-vis the war specifically and the unpleasantness of the world in general, could be referred to as obliteration, which he achieves via alcohol and sex. He is spiritually lost when we meet him, and *A Farewell to Arms* will trace his movement toward an understanding of the world and of himself.

It becomes apparent as soon as they meet that Catherine is different— more mature, in a word—and the characters' contrasting levels of maturity are demonstrated by their different attitudes toward the war. Henry suggests "Let's drop the war." With her characteristic mix of wisdom and humor, Catherine replies, "It's very hard. There's no place to drop it." Permanently scarred by the loss of her fiancé, she already knows that the war can't simply be "dropped."

Additionally, Henry tells us that his declaration of love for Catherine is a lie. "I did not love Catherine Barkley nor had any idea of loving her," he elaborates, comparing their affair to a bridge game. He seems almost boyish at this point in the story, and in a way that isn't necessarily appealing or admirable.

Remember, however, that Henry does not participate in the tormenting of the priest in his unit. He perhaps recognizes that the chaplain stands for something, unlike the cynical, nihilistic officers who taunt him. Henry himself doesn't believe in much of anything yet, but his refusal to join in the ritual of priest-baiting shows us that he respects those who do and that he has potential in this regard. Still, he is uncommitted enough at this point in the story that he can miss an evening with Catherine altogether because he is drinking with his fellow officers. On the other hand, he does regret doing so afterwards. Henry is growing, and growing closer to Catherine.

Just prior to receiving his war wound, Henry is still talking abstractly about bravery (though, significantly, he does admit after the first shelling to being scared). In a bit of foreshadowing that will prove ironic, he argues against giving up: "It would only be worse if we stopped fighting." He says that defeat is worse than war itself. As a result of his own intense pain, however, and the trauma of witnessing of the death of a comrade (not to mention the scene in which he is soaked by the blood of a dying soldier), Henry will no longer be able to deny his involvement in this war or its potential to affect him. He has therefore grown closer to Catherine.

While visiting Henry in the field hospital, the priest tells Henry that the war is made by certain people and executed by others. Henry still resists this notion. He also admits that he does not love God—that perhaps he does not love anyone. "You will," the priest reassures him. "I know you will." Clearly the priest knows Henry better than Henry knows himself. Note the particular nature of the contrast between the peace-loving priest and Henry's roommate Rinaldi, who is warm and likeable but attracted by the violence and sex associated with wartime. At this point in *A Farewell to Arms*, Henry stands somewhere between them, philosophically, as if at a crossroads. It is unclear whose path he will follow, despite his traumatic and painful recent experience.

When Henry and Catherine reunite in Milan, he again declares his love for her—only this time he means it. For Henry, his affair with Catherine is no longer a game, and it is significant that this transformation follows his wounding in battle. The experience has matured Henry, elevating him to a level of wisdom closer to that of Catherine. And yet the dynamic of Henry's naivete versus Catherine's experience and maturity is reiterated as Henry tries to make a date for the night after the operation, and she insists he will be in no shape to see her.

At last Henry's character changes fundamentally during the course of the summer he spends with Catherine; on the heels of his traumatic experience at the front, a love affair with a woman (rather than mere sex with prostitutes) forces him to grow up for good. This change is demonstrated at the start of Chapter XXXIV, after Henry's desertion from the Italian army. Of the hostile aviators with whom he shares a train compartment, he says that "in the old days I would have insulted them and picked a fight." Now, no longer insecure due to his experiences in love and war, he does not even feel insulted. In fact, as his talk with Count Greffi reveals, the once-indifferent Henry has truly found something to believe in. He tells the Count that what he values most is someone he loves and that he "might become very devout," elaborating that his religious feeling comes at night. Like Catherine, Henry has made a religion of their love. For that matter, he has replaced his loyalty to the Italian army with loyalty to Catherine.

In Switzerland, Catherine suggests she and Henry wear their hair the same length, so as to be more alike. "Oh darling," she says, "I want you so much I want to be you too." Henry replies, "You are. We're the same one." And regarding experience and the maturity it yields, he is right. At last Frederic Henry has drawn abreast of Catherine Barkley with respect to wisdom about the world. How has he done so? By participating in love and war, and by making the hard choices that both demand.

When he walks out of the hospital at novel's end, Lieutenant Frederic Henry is a different man than he was at the opening of *A Farewell to Arms*. He has caught up to Catherine Barkley and now understands the world and his place in it. Sadly, he carries that understanding into the rain alone and broken, and forever without her.

Catherine Barkley

Catherine Barkley is a static character in the novel; that is, she does not undergo any major transformation over the course of *A Farewell to Arms*. Apparently she has done her growing and changing before the story began. Hemingway can therefore "use" Catherine as a foil to Henry and an index of his maturation. She is like a constant in a scientific experiment. Of course, this does not make her any less interesting than Henry, and it certainly makes her no less admirable. She's simply less dynamic.

The writer's use of Catherine to contrast dramatically with Henry—to show us just how much learning and growing he has yet to do—begins in the first scene they share together. Henry is still playing childish games: telling her he loves her when he doesn't, for instance. Soon, however, the tables are turned. Catherine not only resists Henry's advances; she reveals that she knows he has been playing a game. Apparently she has been playing one too: "You don't have to pretend you love me," she tells Henry. "You see I'm not mad . . . " Here Catherine proves wiser than she at first appeared—wiser in the ways of the world so far than the easily deceived Henry. Indeed, the latter may be attracted to Catherine precisely because of her aura of hard-earned maturity. Well, that and her hair.

Catherine rejects organized faith, and yet (unlike the priest-baiting officers at the front) she is no nihilist. She lives by a definite, unshakeable value system, and what she values is love. During one of the many nights they spend together in Milan, the couple discusses marriage, which Henry wants but Catherine resists for practical reasons. It would necessitate their separation, she explains—more worldly than he, despite his battlefield experience. She reminds him and us of her having been formally engaged to the soldier who died. Then Catherine tells Henry that she has no religion. She quickly corrects this statement, however, explaining "You're my religion."

Catherine also tells the admitting nurse at the hospital where she goes to give birth at book's end that she lacks a formal religious affiliation of any kind. Henry too calls himself an agnostic, and yet, as virtually anyone would, Henry tries bargaining with God in his desperation at Catherine's impending death. Catherine, on the other hand, retains the courage of her convictions. To the very end, Catherine remains the somewhat stronger of the two. "Just you," she requests of Henry in response to his offer of a priest's visit. Despite everything, love is her religion until the instant she dies.

For much of the novel, Catherine is also more developed than Henry as a Hemingway hero, modest and truthful. Note that while Henry tolerates the "professional hero" Ettore Moretti, Catherine dislikes him intensely. "We have heroes too," Catherine says of Moretti, "But usually, darling, they're much quieter." Additionally, Catherine is distressed by the rigged racetrack betting in which Meyers is involved. "I don't like this crooked racing!" she declares. She suggests to Henry that they bet on a horse they've never heard of, and although it finishes fifth, she feels "so much cleaner." Again, while Henry is tolerant of a certain amount of corruption, Catherine demands purity.

The notion of Catherine's special bravery—another of her heroic qualities—is also introduced during the Milan idyll. With characteristic modesty, she suggests she would like to be brave. When Henry naively suggests that "Nothing ever happens to the brave," the more-experienced Catherine counters with the statement, "They die, of course." And Catherine's extraordinary fortitude is very much in evidence during the escape across Lake Maggiore. Despite her fairly advanced pregnancy, she not only travels through the November night in an open boat but also offers to hold the umbrella so it will serve as a sail. She steers and bails and even rows for a while, always maintaining a sense of humor.

Significantly, we don't doubt Catherine's bravery and stoicism as she perishes; we have been prepared for it by scene after scene in which she displayed just these qualities. What does surprise is her statement, "It's just a dirty trick," which seems to ally her with the cynical, nihilistic officers in Henry's unit. Perhaps Catherine has changed over the course of the novel after all.

CRITICAL ESSAYS

Weather Symbolism

In *A Farewell to Arms*, Ernest Hemingway attempts to tell the unvarnished truth about war—to present an honest, rather than a heroic, account of combat, retreat, and the ways in which soldiers fill their time when they are not fighting. Yet Hemingway's realistic approach to his subject does not rule out the use of many time-honored literary devices.

For instance, weather is to this day a fundamental component of the war experience. Hemingway depicts weather realistically in *A Farewell to Arms*, but he uses it for symbolic purposes as well. Rain, often equated with life and growth, stands for death in this novel, and snow symbolizes hope: an entirely original schema.

Snow

In stories such as "To Build a Fire," by Jack London, snow and ice quite logically represent danger and death. After all, one can freeze to death, fall through thin ice and drown, or perish beneath an avalanche. In Chapter II of *A Farewell Arms*, on the other hand, it is snow that ends the fighting described in the book's first chapter. Thus snow stands for safety rather than its opposite. (Note, though, that although snow covers the bare ground and even the Italian army's artillery in Chapter II, stumps of oak trees torn up by the summer's fighting continue to protrude—a reminder that winter is of course not permanent but merely a reprieve from combat, a cease-fire.) Shortly thereafter, Frederic Henry describes the priest's home region of Abruzzi as a "place where the roads were frozen and hard as iron, where it was clear and cold and dry and the snow was dry and powdery . . . ," and the context leaves no doubt that this characterization is a positive one.

Late in the novel, the argument between the Swiss policemen over winter sports not only provides much-needed comic relief; it also marks the beginning of Henry and Catherine Barkley's second idyll. (The first takes place in summertime, in Milan.) Immediately afterwards, Henry and Catherine find themselves in the Swiss Alps, with snow all around. Thus they have temporarily achieved a life of both purity (the mountains symbolize purity in this novel, versus the corruption of the lowlands) and safety. These chapters positively radiate contentment.

Rain

Starting in the very first chapter of *A Farewell to Arms*, rain clearly symbolizes death: "In the fall when the rains came the leaves all fell from the chestnut trees and the branches were bare and the trunks black with rain," Henry tells us. "The vineyards were thin and bare-branched too and all the country wet and brown and dead with autumn." The rain symbolism is not entirely a literary conceit, either, as rain actually precedes an outbreak of fatal illness, the cholera that kills seven thousand that fall.

Later, during their Milan idyll, Catherine makes the symbolism of the rain explicit for Henry—and for the reader: "I'm afraid of the rain because sometimes I see myself dead in it," she says to him. "And sometimes I see you dead in it." Lo and behold, during Henry and Catherine's trip from the armorer's to the hotel near the train station on his last night with her, the fog that has covered the city from the start of the chapter turns to rain. It continues to rain as they bid one another farewell; in fact, Catherine's last act in this part of the novel is to signal to Henry that he should step in out of the rain. Back at the front, "the trees were all bare and the roads were muddy."

It rains almost continuously during the chapter when the tide of battle turns and the Italians begin their retreat from Caporetto—and from the Germans who have joined the fighting. The rain turns to snow one evening, holding out hope that the offensive will cease, but the snow quickly melts and the rain resumes. During a discussion among the drivers about the wine they are drinking with dinner, the driver named Aymo says, "To-morrow maybe we drink rainwater." Hemingway by this time has developed the rain symbolism to such a degree that the reader experiences a genuine sense of foreboding—and indeed, the following day will bring death to Henry's disintegrating unit.

It is raining while the fugitive Henry rides the train to Stresa, raining when he arrives, and raining while Henry and Catherine spend the night together in his hotel room. The open-boat trip across Lake Maggiore takes place in the rain, with an umbrella used as a sail. (Ominously, the umbrella breaks.) And in Chapter XL, as Henry and Catherine are bidding farewell to their wintertime mountain retreat for the city in which Catherine's baby is to be born, Henry tells us that "In the night it started raining."

Finally, when Henry leaves the hospital for lunch during Catherine's protracted, agonizing delivery, "The day was cloudy but the sun was trying to come through"—a literal ray of hope. During the operation, however, he looks out the window and sees that it is raining. Just after the nurse has told him that the baby is dead, Henry looks outside again and "could see nothing but the dark and the rain falling across the light from the window." At the novel's end, Henry leaves the hospital and walks back to his hotel in the rain. In fact, the final word in *A Farewell to Arms* is "rain," evidence of weather's important place in the story overall.

Hemingway doesn't quite trust us to detect the rain/snow pattern of symbolism and understand its meaning; therefore he underlines the significance of precipitation in his book by having Catherine tell Henry that she sees them dead in the rain. And so the weather symbolism in *A Farewell to Arms* is perhaps unnecessarily obvious. Yet Hemingway's use of this literary device is hardly rote symbolism for its own sake. Rain and snow both drive his plot and maintain our interest, as we hold our breaths every time it rains in the novel, praying that Catherine will not perish during that scene. (We know that Henry will survive the rain, because he is the story's narrator.) Thus, while writing a brutally realistic saga of life during wartime, Ernest Hemingway also crafted a novel as literary as the great-war stories that preceded *A Farewell to Arms*. Arguably it is as powerful as any story ever told.

The Hemingway Influence

Ernest Hemingway has been called the twentieth century's most influential writer. With the publication of *A Farewell to Arms* in 1929, he achieved widespread fame, and despite a steady decline in the quality of his work thereafter, his fame continued to grow until his suicide in 1961 and beyond. Striking evidence of this is the 1958 movie of *The Old Man and the Sea*; it's hard to imagine a book less suited to the big screen, and yet Hemingway's celebrity at the time of its publication was so massive that Hollywood had virtually no choice but to film the novella. The publication of recovered fragments from the writer's unpublished *oeuvre* has never failed to make headlines worldwide, from *A Moveable Feast* in 1964 to the so-called "fictional memoir" *True at First Light*, in 1999. Like those of Shakespeare and Einstein, Hemingway's face is recognized by millions who have never read a word he wrote.

Hemingway achieved more than celebrity, however. If imitation is the sincerest form of flattery, then he was a great writer indeed.

Especially after reading *A Farewell to Arms*, Hemingway's influence is easy to discern in an enormous number of the writers who have followed him. This influence has taken three forms: thematic, stylistic, and the "Papa" Hemingway lifestyle.

The Hemingway Character

As the literary critic Leslie Fiedler argues in his study *Love and Death in the American Novel*, the classic American literary hero is a soldier, sailor, or cowboy who is brave, laconic, and (ultimately) alone. From Hawkeye in James Fenimore Cooper's *Last of the Mohicans* through *Moby-Dick*'s Ishmael and Mark Twain's Huckleberry Finn, these characters "light out for the territories" because they don't quite fit in polite society, and they quickly learn self-sufficiency in the wilderness, at sea, or in combat. Hemingway, who identified *Adventures of Huckleberry Finn* as the source of all American literature, recognized this archetype, then updated and refined it. The overriding theme of his stories and books was "grace under pressure"—specifically, the ability of "men without women" (the title of an early story collection) to remain calm and competent in the face of life-threatening violence.

Thus, Hemingway heroes like Frederic Henry stoically accept not only war wounds, but the pain of losing whom they love, as well. (Think of Henry walking into the rain after the agonizing death of his lover and child at the conclusion of *A Farewell to Arms*.) Whether handling firearms, betting on horses, or ordering wine, they are almost scarily adept at what they do, and when the universe conspires to defeat them, they never complain.

The influence of the Hemingway hero can therefore be seen in many of the literary soldiers who followed in Henry's footsteps: for instance, the protagonist of James Salter's *The Hunters*, an account of the exploits of a Korean War jet pilot squadron. It is even more evident in the archetypal tough-talking detectives of Raymond Chandler (*The Big Sleep*) and James Ellroy (*L.A. Confidential*). (Note: Like Frederic Henry, Chandler's protagonist Philip Marlowe is a veteran of World War I, as evinced by his trademark trenchcoat—the coat worn by Allied officers in the trenches of France and Italy. Nearly every character Humphrey Bogart ever played onscreen was influenced by the Hemingway hero.) The cowboys in Cormac McCarthy's *Border Trilogy* are essentially Hemingway characters, too.

The Hemingway Style

Hemingway's influence has been even more pronounced in the realm of prose style. In his first collection of stories and thereafter, he combined elements from Gertrude Stein, James Joyce, and journalism to create a radically modern approach to the writing of sentences and paragraphs distinguished by the following hallmarks:

■ *An emphasis on nouns and verbs rather than adjectives and adverbs.* This is closely related to Hemingway's preference for the actual versus the abstract. "I was always embarrassed by the words sacred, glorious, and sacrifice and the expression in vain," Frederic Henry tells us in *A Farewell to Arms*. "Abstract words such as glory, honor, courage or hallow were obscene beside the concrete names of villages, the numbers of roads, the names of rivers, the numbers of regiments and the dates."

■ *A limited word-palette.* Hemingway was fluent in three romance languages: French, Spanish, and Italian. Each has a much smaller vocabulary than English, and yet each manages to be richly expressive. Hemingway may have been inspired by this phenomenon.

■ *Frequent repetition of the same words and phrases*—a technique learned from Gertrude Stein. (The best known sentences she ever wrote were "A rose is a rose is a rose" and "When you get there, there's no there there.")

■ *Short sentences* ("The next year there were many victories.") *or long sentences consisting of short phrases and clauses connected by conjunctions*: "The mountain that was beyond the valley and the hillside where the chestnut forest grew was captured and there were victories beyond the plain on the plateau to the south and we crossed the river in August and lived in a house in Gorizia that had a fountain and many thick shady trees in a walled garden and a wistaria vine purple on the side of the house." (*A Farewell to Arms*, Chapter II)

■ *A lack of clarity in the relationship between one sentence and the next.* Instead of writing "I drank much wine because it was good," Hemingway writes "The wine was good. I drank much of it," merely implying the relationship. He thus forces us to be active readers, connecting the dots and filling in the blanks.

Many storytellers (Salter, Chandler, McCarthy, and others) have attempted to recapitulate Hemingway's themes while mimicking his prose style. During the 1970s and 1980s, however, a group of American writers known as the Minimalists adopted the Hemingway style but rejected "grace under pressure" and so forth as distasteful and perhaps permanently outdated.

In her earliest stories, Ann Beattie wrote in the Hemingway style about well-off Baby Boomers paralyzed by the challenges of adulthood. (Like Chandler and so many others, Beattie has specifically mentioned Hemingway as an inspiration, specifically the inter-chapter vignettes from *In Our Time*.) Raymond Carver's down-and-out drunks could hardly be less heroic, and yet the use of diction and syntax in his masterly short stories is profoundly indebted to Hemingway. Frederick Barthelme continues to craft stories and novels in an intentionally flat, unadorned voice about largely ineffectual men (and sexy, aggressive women) living in the so-called New South. All these writers jettisoned the sometimes embarrassing excesses associated with Hemingway's value system while retaining the lessons he taught them as a writer of prose.

The Hemingway Lifestyle

Finally, in many ways Ernest Hemingway exemplified for the Twentieth Century what it means to live like a writer. The most visible example of his influence in this area has been Norman Mailer. Though Mailer's often baroque style could hardly be more different from Hemingway's (an exception is the laconic "non-fiction novel" *The Executioner's Song*, which many critics consider Mailer's best book), he seems to have modeled his life after Hemingway's, seeking fistfights, serial wives (Hemingway had four, Mailer six), and "Papa"-like celebrity in general. And the career of the George Plimpton has been a kind of parody of Hemingway's: Plimpton lived in Paris as a young man, but founded a magazine rather than writing stories and novels. Since then he has engaged in a number of stunts that seem actually to mock Hemingway's vigorous lifestyle while attempting to pay it tribute: briefly fighting a champion boxer and playing professional football, for instance, then writing books about the experiences.

Prior to the publication of *A Farewell to Arms*, the Romantic poets probably served as our primary model for the writing life. A writer was a tortured soul recollecting his or her experiences in tranquility, *a la* Wordsworth, Shelley, and Keats. Hemingway changed all that. Proust composed *Remembrance of Things Past* in bed; Hemingway wrote standing up. Then he went big-game hunting or deep-sea fishing, or to the bullfights.

Today, Hemingway's thematic influence is a victim of its own success. The tough-talking private investigator is such a pervasive figure in our culture that is seems always to have existed. As his death recedes further into the past, the "Papa" lifestyle becomes harder to recall—and therefore tougher to emulate than when Hemingway's exploits were a fixture in newsreels and the pages of *Life* magazine. Regarding the influence of his prose itself, however, the Nobel Prize committee was correct when it rewarded Ernest Hemingway "for his powerful, style-forming mastery of the art of narration." He changed the way we write and read literature, and he changed it forever.

CliffsNotes Review

Use this CliffsNotes Review to test your understanding of the original text and reinforce what you've learned in this book. After you work through the review and essay questions, identify the quote section, and the fun and useful practice projects, you're well on your way to understanding a comprehensive and meaningful interpretation of *A Farewell to Arms*.

Q&A

1. *A Farewell to Arms* takes place during World War I in _____, _____, and _____.

2. The novel's protagonist, the American Frederic Henry, is a second lieutenant in the army of _____.

3. During the course of the book, this army opposes the forces of _____ and _____.

4. Henry's lover, nurse Catherine Barkley, is a native of _____.

5. The main geographical dichotomy in the book is the contrast between _____ and _____.

6. Henry supervises a group of _____.

7. Henry is wounded most severely in the _____.

8. Both Lieutenant Henry and Catherine Barkley are sent to an American hospital in _____.

9. Henry is afraid of _____.

10. Catherine is afraid of _____.

11. During the Battle of Caporetto, _____ enter the fighting.

12. The pistol Henry buys in Milan is used to _____.

13. Henry deserts from the Italian army when he _____.

14. Henry and Catherine flee across Lake Maggiore into _____.

15. Frederic and Catherine's baby is _____.

Answers: (1) Italy, Austria, Switzerland (2) Italy (3) The Austro-Hungarian Empire, Germany (4) Great Britain (Scotland) (5) Mountains, plains (6) Ambulance drivers and mechanics (7) Leg (8) Milan (9) The dark (10) The rain (11) Germans (12) Kill a deserter (13) Dives into a river and swims away (14) Switzerland (15) Stillborn

Identify the Quote

1. One side must stop fighting. Why don't we stop fighting? If they come down into Italy they will get tired and go away. But no, instead there is a war.

2. You'll never get married . . . . You'll fight before you marry . . . . You'll die then. Fight or die. That's what people do . . . . Maybe you'll be all right, you two. But watch out you don't get her in trouble. You get her in trouble and I'll kill you . . . . I don't want her with any of those war babies.

3. I'm afraid of the rain because sometimes I see myself dead in it . . . . And sometimes I see you dead in it."

4. I was always embarrassed by the words sacred, glorious, and sacrifice and the expression in vain. Abstract words such as glory, honor, courage or hallow were obscene beside the concrete names of villages, the numbers of roads, the names of rivers, the numbers of regiments and the dates."

5. If people bring so much courage to the world that the world has to kill them to break them, so of course it kills them. The world breaks everyone and afterward many are strong at the broken places. But those that will not break it kills. It kills the very good and the very gentle and the very brave impartially. If you are none of these you can be sure it will kill you too but there will be no special hurry."

Answers: (1) [Passini to the other ambulance drivers and mechanics, just before the Austrian bombardment that kills him. This speech may plant the idea of desertion in Lieutenant Henry's head.] (2) [Helen Ferguson to Lieutenant Henry, in the American hospital in Milan. Ferguson's prediction proves partly correct, partly incorrect, as Henry and Catherine don't fight, but she does die. Their "war baby" will be stillborn.] (3) [Catherine Barkley to Lieutenant Henry, in Milan. More foreshadowing, which increases dramatic tension and encourages us to read on. Furthermore, every time it rains in the novel, we will worry for Catherine and Henry.] (4) [Henry to the reader. This quote not only characterizes the Lieutenant; it also serves as Hemingway's stylistic credo.] (5) [Henry to the reader. The most famous passage *A Farewell to Arms*, this quote undeniably foreshadows the book's end: Catherine is too strong to live, and thus she must be "broken" and die.]

Essay Questions

1. How effective are the opening chapters of *A Farewell to Arms*? What makes them effective/ineffective?

2. Write an essay discussing Hemingway's use of lowlands and mountains as symbols.

3. Compare and contrast the novel's most significant supporting characters: Rinaldi and the priest.

4. Are Henry's reasons for deserting the Italian army convincing? Why or why not?

5. Compare the novel's two idyllic sections: the summer spent in Milan and the winter in Switzerland.

6. Compare and contrast Italy and Switzerland in general, as they appear in this novel.

7. Write an essay in which you disagree with the truism that the essential Hemingway style is typified by short, declarative sentence.

8. Ernest Hemingway has been accused of sexism. Is Catherine Barkley a believable, three-dimensional character? What about the other female characters in *A Farewell to Arms*?

9. Is Hemingway's treatment of the love between Henry and Catherine too much or not enough?

10. Write an essay about the common man in *A Farewell to Arms*.

Practice Projects

1. Imagine that you are writing a screenplay for a two-hour movie of *A Farewell to Arms*. You are limited to about 120 script pages. Which of the novel's scenes, characters, and events would you include and exclude?

2. Prepare a meal featuring food and drink mentioned in *A Farewell to Arms*.

3. Use an atlas to compose an itinerary for *A Farewell to Arms* vacation, starting near the Slovenian border in northeast Italy, traveling across the country to Milan by train and then up into Switzerland via Lake Maggiore.

CliffsNotes Resource Center

The learning doesn't need to stop here. CliffsNotes Resource Center shows you the best of the best—links to the best information in print and online about the author and/or related works. And don't think that this is all we've prepared for you; we've put all kinds of pertinent information at www.cliffsnotes.com. Look for all the terrific resources at your favorite bookstore or local library and on the Internet. When you're online, make your first stop www.cliffsnotes.com where you'll find more incredibly useful information about *A Farewell to Arms*.

Books

This CliffsNotes book provides a meaningful interpretation of *A Farewell to Arms*. If you are looking for information about the author and/or related works, check out these other publications:

Hemingway, by Carlos Baker. This massive study by an acclaimed scholar of American literature and acknowledged Hemingway expert stresses the use of symbolism throughout the writer's work. Princeton: Princeton University Press, 1972.

Along With Youth: Hemingway the Early Years, by Peter Griffin. A brief and perhaps too-worshipful tour through Hemingway's boyhood, adolescence, and young manhood, this book is nevertheless valuable for its in-depth examination of his ill-fated relationship with Agnes von Kurowski, the model for Catherine Barkley in *A Farewell to Arms.* (Griffin's reconstruction of the day on which Hemingway received the letter that ended the affair is truly heartbreaking.) Sometimes the author naively confuses the stories and novels with the events that inspired them, but *Along With Youth* contains generous quotations from many letters to and from Hemingway, as well as a large selection of family photographs. Oxford: Oxford University Press, 1985.

The Complete Stories: The Finca Vigia Edition, by Ernest Hemingway. This definitive collection contains stories of postwar trauma like "Soldier's Home" and "Big Two-Hearted River" helpful in understanding Hemingway's attitude toward World War I and its aftermath. New York: Charles Scribner's Sons, 1987.

Hemingway: A Biography, by Jeffrey Meyers. This biography is exhaustive but never fawning, and while it offers interpretations of the writer's *oeuvre,* they are reasonable and unforced. Meyers sees Hemingway's life for the tragedy it was, and he refuses to flinch from the depressing fact that the author's work began to decline in quality almost immediately following the publication of *A Farewell to Arms.* This book also contains a fascinating, if bizarre, appendix listing the writer's many accidents and injuries, including, of course, the injury that inspired *A Farewell to Arms.* Cambridge, MA: Da Capo, 1999.

Ernest Hemingway, Dateline: Toronto, edited by William Whyte. One major tributary feeding the Hemingway prose style was his training as a journalist. This book collects the Hemingway's dispatches from Europe during the early Twenties. New York: Charles Scribner's Sons, 1985.

It's easy to find books published by Wiley Publishing, Inc. You'll find them in your favorite bookstores (on the Internet and at a store near you). We also have three Web sites that you can use to read about all the books we publish:

■ www.cliffsnotes.com

■ www.dummies.com

■ www.wiley.com

Internet

Check out these Web resources for more information about Ernest Hemingway and *A Farewell to Arms*:

Ernest Hemingway's Kansas City Star Stories, kcstar.com/about-star/hemingway/ernie.htm—A collection of the articles written by Hemingway for the *Kansas City Star* during World War I, prior to his departure for Italy.

Hemingway Resource Center, www.lostgeneration.com/hrc.htm—This excellent Web site includes a biography, a bibliography, a message board, and links to other Hemingway-related sites.

"Picturing Hemingway: A Writer in His Time," www.npg.si.edu/exh/hemingway/index.htm—An online version of a 1999 exhibit at the National Portrait Gallery, which includes a photo of Hemingway in his World War I ambulance driver's uniform as well as one of Agnes von Kurowsky in her nurse's outfit.

Tour of the Hemingway Birthhome in Oak Park, Illinois, www.oprf. com/Hemingway/tour/—A virtual tour of Hemingway's Oak Park home, including blueprints of the house and details of its restoration undertaken by the Ernest Hemingway Foundation of Oak Park.

Tracking Hemingway, www.theatlantic.com/unbound/flashbks/ hemingway.htm—This site contains *Atlantic Monthly* articles, essays, and reviews on Hemingway, published from 1939 to 1983 and written by Edmund Wilson, Malcolm Cowley, Alfred Kazin, and other esteemed critics.

Next time you're on the Internet, don't forget to drop by www. cliffsnotes.com. We created an online Resource Center that you can use today, tomorrow, and beyond.

Films and Other Recordings

Following are films and a recording you may find interesting additions to your study of Hemingway and *A Farewell to Arms*:

A Farewell to Arms, Paramount, 1932. The first of three films inspired by the bestselling novel butchers Hemingway's story in the process of condensing it to just over an hour in length. There are substantial changes as well as omissions: Catherine flees alone to Switzerland, Rinaldi is a sort of antagonist who intercepts her letters and Frederic's, and the movie ends with the signing of the armistice. Most absurdly of all, at least to a contemporary sensibility, Frederic and Catherine are secretly married while he lies in bed in the hospital in Milan. This film illustrates by contrast just how subtle the novel itself was—not to mention groundbreaking, with respect to morality. Directed by Frank Borzage and starring Gary Cooper and Helen Hayes.

Ernest Hemingway Reading, Caedmon, Mono 41-7222, 1965. This tape includes a recording of the author reading his Nobel Prize acceptance speech, as well as a handful of fragments and a poem to his fourth wife. The flat, largely uninflected quality of Hemingway's midwestern accent suggests that what he sought on the printed page was an approximation of the sound of his own speaking voice.

Michael Palin's Hemingway Adventure, PBS Home Video, 2000. In this delightful set of tapes, originally a public television series, a former member of the Monty Python comedy troupe lives out his boyhood fantasy by retracing Papa's steps. He studies bullfighting in Spain, tracks big game in Africa, drinks in a Havana bar—and drives an Italian ambulance, visiting the exact spot where Hemingway was wounded during World War I. These videos are refreshingly unpretentious and as willing to poke fun at their subject as to appreciate the challenges inherent in living his vigorous life. Directed by David F. Turnbull.

A Farewell to Arms, TCF, 1957. Hollywood's third version of the novel, rewritten for the screen by the otherwise masterful Ben Hecht, tried to transform it into a sort of epic adventure story. Directed by David O. Selznick and starring Rock Hudson and Jennifer Jones.

Magazines and Journals

Atlas, James. "Papa Lives." *The Atlantic Monthly,* October 1983. www. theatlantic.com/issues/83oct/8310atlas.htm—A clear-eyed reassessment of four Hemingway novels (*The Sun Also Rises, A Farewell to Arms, For Whom the Bell Tolls,* and *The Old Man and the Sea*) upon their reissue. Atlas acknowledges the author's weaknesses while celebrating his strengths and argues convincingly that Hemingway remains one of the Twentieth Century's greatest writers.

Send Us Your Favorite Tips

In your quest for knowledge, have you ever experienced that sublime moment when you figure out a trick that saves time or trouble? Perhaps you realized you were taking ten steps to accomplish something that could have taken two. Or you found a little-known workaround that achieved great results. If you've discovered a useful resource that gave you insight into or helped you understand *A Farewell to Arms* and you'd like to share it, the CliffsNotes staff would love to hear from you. Go to our Web site at www.cliffsnotes.com and click the Talk to Us button. If we select your tip, we may publish it as part of CliffsNotes Daily, our exciting, free e-mail newsletter. To find out more or to subscribe to a newsletter, go to www.cliffsnotes.com on the Web.

Index

NOTES

NOTES

NOTES

CliffsN☺tes™
@ cliffsnotes.com

Check Out the All-New CliffsNotes Guides